T0384187

'Lori Brown and Alison Bartlett have created a useable text that provides practical trauma-informed strategies that support both students and teachers in the creation of a trauma-informed school. The authors have insightfully included a whole chapter not just on cultural competencies but also on cultural humility. In an ever changing world, we must all be aware of our own cultural biases. This is a must read for all teachers.'

Coreen Collins, *Manager Student Support, Department of Education, Government of Nunavut*

'As our youngest students experience trauma around them, we as the adults who care for them and educate them, must be better prepared to understand the natural responses of children to the trauma in their lives. Lori Brown, Psy.D is an authority on this topic and has written a very readable, research informed, guide to the steps a school community can take to ensure that the entire school community is prepared to support and work with all students.'

Rebecca Wardlow, *EdD, Dean, College of Education, United States University*

'This book addresses important issues in education today, such as how trauma happens to individuals and cultures, as well as how to address it in your classrooms. Written for teachers by teachers, it is a thoroughly researched and user-friendly resource for education in 21st century. Well done!'

Armand Doucet C.M., *High School Teacher, New Brunswick, Canada*

Trauma-Informed Teaching in Your Elementary Classroom

Research has proven that childhood trauma affects school engagement and success while at the same time recognizing that the majority of students have experienced it. This book offers simple strategies, based on evidence-based studies, that elementary educators can use to effectively recognize trauma, teach resilience, and support their students in being ready to learn. The book covers all the tenets of trauma-informed teaching, including understanding the effects of trauma, creating safety and predictability, fostering healthy attachments, and modeling resilience as part of social emotional learning, all of which are framed within cultural humility and competence. Designed for all teachers, professionals, and school administrators working with elementary students, this practical guide is key reading for creating a safe classroom and school environment that is inclusive of all learners and conducive for learning.

Lori Brown, Psy.D. has 28 years of experience working as a teacher, registrar, counselor, administrator, and consultant in the public school system.

Alison Bartlett, B.Ed. has worked in the Anglophone East School District since 1989 as a classroom teacher and had a Special Position of Responsibility (SPR) for her school's Positive Learning Environment.

Trauma-Informed Teaching in Your Elementary Classroom

Simple Strategies to Create Inclusive, Safe Spaces as the First Step to Learning

Lori Brown, Psy.D. and Alison Bartlett, B.Ed.

Routledge
Taylor & Francis Group

NEW YORK AND LONDON

Designed cover image: Getty Images

First published 2025
by Routledge
605 Third Avenue, New York, NY 10158

and by Routledge
4 Park Square, Milton Park, Abingdon, Oxon, OX14 4RN

Routledge is an imprint of the Taylor & Francis Group, an informa business

© 2025 Taylor & Francis

The right of Lori Brown and Alison Bartlett to be identified as authors of this work has been asserted in accordance with sections 77 and 78 of the Copyright, Designs and Patents Act 1988.

ISBN: 978-1-032-70793-8 (hbk)
ISBN: 978-1-032-68676-9 (pbk)
ISBN: 978-1-032-70794-5 (ebk)

DOI: 10.4324/9781032707945

Typeset in Palatino
by SPi Technologies India Pvt Ltd (Straive)

Contents

Meet the Authors

Lori Brown, B.Sc., B.Ed., M.Ed. (Counseling), M.Ed. (Diverse Learners), Psy.D. has 28 years of experience working as a teacher, registrar, counselor, administrator, and consultant in the public school system. Lori's doctoral work includes a systematic review of 135 recent research articles addressing the psychological repercussions of childhood trauma, academic effects, and components of school-based programming implemented to meet the needs of affected youth while creating resilience.

Alison Bartlett, B.Sc., B.Ed. has worked in the Anglophone East School District since 1989 as a classroom teacher and was the SPR for her school's Positive Learning Environment. She has edited educational documents read by teachers worldwide. She was a recipient of the NB Minister's Excellence in Teaching Award.

Introduction

One goal of education, in addition to teaching the curriculum, is to assist our students in reaching their full potential. This means that they can march into adulthood armed with a variety of skills and knowledge and become contributing members of society. In this book, we will address an issue that can drastically reduce the likelihood of that happening. That issue is trauma. You will read about the impact that exposure to trauma has on your students, and you will learn strategies that ultimately help these children help themselves so that they do more than merely limp into adulthood.

At its core, trauma is an experience so horrible that your mind and body never let you forget. Traumatic events include, but sadly are not limited to, natural disasters, terrorism, war, poverty, domestic or community violence, neglect, emotional, physical, and sexual abuse, disease or injuries, and the death of a loved one (Fratto, 2016). In March of 2020, we added the COVID pandemic to this list.

We all carry trauma. However, it is important to remember that trauma comes in a variety of forms, and we each manifest our trauma differently. Therefore, a variety of behaviors may be observed in your classroom, such as symptoms of attention deficit disorder with hyperactivity, conduct disorder, oppositional defiant disorder, reactive attachment disorder, or acute stress

DOI: 10.4324/9781032707945-1

disorders (Brunzell et al., 2016). Even generalized disruptive behaviors can be an expression of fear, sadness, or grief. Hence, you need to be aware of alternate perspectives that consider evidence-based research in trauma-informed practice (Wesseley et al., 2008).

Remember this acronym: ACEs (Adverse Childhood Experiences). Exposures to ACEs affect the structure and function of the developing brain, specifically the amygdala, hippocampus, and prefrontal cortex. Such damage impairs a child's social, emotional, and cognitive development (Lang, 2016). These impairments result in difficulties regulating emotions and behaviors (Jaycox et al., 2012). In other words, trauma affects the brain and the nervous system in ways that prevent an individual's capacity for developing healthy attachments to others (Siegel et al., 2012). The ACE questionnaire is called the Adverse Childhood Experiences Questionnaire.[1] If you have a hard copy of our book, follow these steps:

Step 1: Go to www.camh.ca.
Step 2: Go to the search icon and type in 'ACE questionnaire'.
Step 3: Select the option entitled 'Adverse Childhood Experiences Questionnaire'. (*Adverse Childhood Experiences Questionnaire*, 2018)

By the way, adults with four or more ACEs are much more likely to develop depression and to use alcohol and drugs. According to the Centers for Disease Control and Prevention (CDC), 1 in 6 people suffer four or more traumatizing events in their lives (Centers for Disease Control, 2023).

The CDC has a stellar section within its Violence Prevention homepage.[2] If you have a hard copy of our book, follow these steps:

Step 1: Go to cdc.gov.
Step 2: In the search bar, type in 'Adverse Childhood Experiences' (Centre for Addiction and Mental Health, 2018).

Not surprisingly, scoring 4 or higher on the ACE survey related to increased incidents with law enforcement, homelessness, and decreased employability.

The original ACE study,[3] in 1994, assessed the relationship between household abuse/dysfunction and increased risky behaviors later in life. If you have a hard copy of our book, follow these steps:

Step 1: Google search 'Relationships of Childhood Abuse and Household Dysfunction to Many of the Leading Causes of Death in Adults: The Adverse Childhood Experiences Study.'

Step 2: Click on the *American Journal of Preventive Medicine* link.

The first ACE pyramid looked like this:

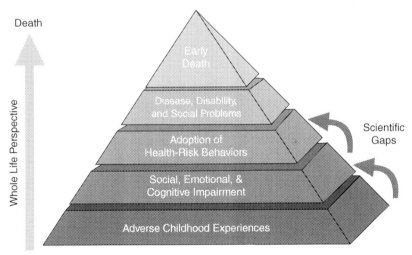

FIGURE 0.1 ACE Pyramid

Source: Centers for Disease Control and Prevention, 2023

Unlike high school, elementary school children spend much of their day with one person: You. This is why your room is the best place to recognize and respond to ACEs (Bruhn et al., 2014). Research shows that trauma-informed approaches to teaching have resulted in links between healthy social and emotional functioning of students and their academic success (Overstreet & Chafouleas, 2016). Specifically, cognitive-behavioral strategies that can be learned, supported, and practiced at school can create a more positive trajectory for students affected by ACEs. The acquisition of these strategies can improve emotional regulation, interpersonal communication, attachments to others, and academic success.

That, in a nutshell, describes where we are going in this book. In Part 1, 'The Why,' we will examine the causes and effects of trauma for individuals and across generations. In Part 2, 'The How,' we will look at how to ensure culturally diverse learners are not marginalized in our increasingly diverse classrooms, as well as how you can unshackle your students from the trauma-induced stress response affecting their learning. We will also take some time to address your own wellness.

We have added 'Resources' lists at the end of Chapters 3 and 5, which we hope you find helpful. We are adding 'nuggets' for you to gather as you read the book. We consider the nuggets as being especially salient highlights. Further, we have embedded links to websites to look through and YouTube videos to watch. They are extensions of the content and an opportunity to gain deeper insights and solidify your knowledge before moving on. Know that we have been judicious in selecting them. There are three in this introduction. Did you look at them? We have also added 'brain breaks.' You may be inclined to think of them as little assignments (*groan*). You will find the answers to the brain breaks directly after each chapter.

By availing yourself of all the opportunities in this book, you will have a much more thorough understanding of trauma, its causes, its effects, and, most importantly, what you can do to help your students overcome them.

Notes

1 https://www.camh.ca/-/media/files/professionals/childhood-trauma-toolkit/ace-questionnaire-2018-pdf.pdf.
2 https://www.cdc.gov/violenceprevention/aces/fastfact.html.
3 https://www.ajpmonline.org/article/S0749-3797(98)00017-8/fulltext.

References

Bruhn, A. L., Woods-Groves, S., & Huddle, S. (2014). A preliminary investigation of emotional and behavioral screening practices in K–12 schools. *Education and Treatment of Children, 37*(4), 611–634. https://doi.org/10.1353/etc.2014.0039

Brunzell, T., Stokes, H., & Waters, L. (2016). Trauma-informed positive education: Using positive psychology to strengthen vulnerable students. *Contemporary School Psychology, 20*(1), 63–83. https://doi.org/10.1007/s40688-015-0070-x

Centers for Disease Control. (2023). *Fast facts: Preventing adverse childhood experiences.* https://www.cdc.gov/violenceprevention/aces/fastfact.html

Centre for Addiction and Mental Health. (2018). *Adverse childhood experiences questionnaire.* https://www.camh.ca/-/media/images/professionals/pdfs/ace-questionnaire-2018-pdf.pdf

Fratto, C. M. (2016). Trauma-informed care for youth in foster care. *Archives of Psychiatric Nursing, 30*(3), 439–446. https://www.psychiatricnursing.org/article/S0883-9417(16)00017-0/fulltext

Jaycox, L., Kataoka, S.; Stein, B., Langley, A., & Wong, M. (2012). Cognitive behavioral intervention for trauma in schools. *Journal of Applied School Psychology,* 239–255. https://doi.org/10.1080/15377903.2012.695766

Lang, J. M. (2016). *Small teaching: Everyday lessons from the science of learning.* John Wiley & Sons.

Overstreet, S., & Chafouleas, S. M. (2016). Trauma-informed schools: Introduction to the special issue. *School Mental Health, 8,* 1–6. https://doi.org/10.1007/s12310-016-9184-1

Siegel, B., Dobbins, M., Earls, M., Andrew, S., Garner, A., McGuinn, L., Pascoe, J., & Wood, D. (2012). The lifelong effects of early childhood adversity and toxic stress. *Pediatrics, 29*(1) 232–246. https://doi.org/10.1542/peds.2011-2663

Wessely, S., Bryant, R. A., Greenberg, N., Earnshaw, M., Sharpley, J., & Hughes, J. H. (2008). Does psychoeducation help prevent post traumatic psychological distress? *Psychiatry, 71*(4), 287–302. https://doi.org/10.1521/psyc.2008.71.4.287

Part 1
The Why

1

Understanding Trauma

Kelly is a grade 3 student. At the grade 3 school team meeting, Kelly's art teacher, Ms. Simpson, raised a concern about Kelly's explosive behaviors in recent weeks. During a 'Create a Family Thanksgiving Comic Book' assignment, Kelly smashed her pencil on the table, kicked over a chair, and screamed profanities. The explosive behavior was not just disruptive but also quite upsetting to the young classmates who had been working quietly. The teacher spoke to Kelly about the effect her behavior had on others in the room and that if it happened again, she would be phoning home. The following day, Kelly repeated the same behavior and then bolted from the room. Ms. Simpson thought that because art class was just before lunch, perhaps Kelly had left the building. The school guidance counselor, who happened to live in the same neighborhood as Kelly's family, informed the school team that Kelly's mother had recently remarried.

Mrs. Jackson, the Language Arts teacher, spoke next. She stated that Kelly had appeared tired and distracted. She had observed that Kelly's face had become flushed and that her jaw tightened, her breathing rate increased, and she seemed to be perspiring. She told Kelly's other teachers that she had crouched beside Kelly's desk, spoken to her in soothing words, and told her that everything was going to be okay. She told Kelly that she could decide for herself if/when she needed to go to the nook

DOI: 10.4324/9781032707945-3

at the back of the room and have some alone time. At the beginning of the year, Mrs. Jackson had set up a little table with headphones, crayons, paper, and Play-Doh. Mrs. Jackson said that in the few days after she spoke to Kelly, she noticed that Kelly had done just that. Occasionally, she had quietly put her classwork down and went to the nook. There, she put on the noise-canceling headphones and used the Play-Doh to make colorful shapes. Mrs. Jackson monitored Kelly closely and prompted her to return to her seat when she appeared more at ease.

Tania, the school counselor, began collecting information to help Kelly and her teachers. She visited Kelly's teachers the next day to get some insights. Ms. Simpson, the art teacher, said, 'Kelly knows the rules of the classroom. I cannot have a student upsetting her classmates and disrupting my lesson. There needs to be consequences for her behavior.' The conversation with the Language Arts teacher, Mrs. Jackson, was different. 'I know when Kelly starts to become dysregulated because she stops concentrating on her work, I see that her face becomes flushed, her muscles tighten a bit and she appears as if she's going to cry or blow up.' Mrs. Jackson adds,

I know that Kelly would not want to behave explosively in front of her peers. I have a close relationship with Kelly. I see her dysregulation ease down when I speak to her with soothing words, make eye contact with her, and give her some control.

When Tania phoned home, Kelly's mother answered the phone, speaking in a hushed voice. Tania heard a man yelling in the background. Sensing distress, Tania asked Kelly's mother if she could visit the school, alone, for a cup of coffee and a chat.

As you read through this chapter, you will gain a solid understanding of trauma so that you can truly understand what some of your students, like Kelly, are going through when triggered at school. In this way, you can choose the best strategy to help them. You will need a basic understanding of the human nervous system, particularly the human brain. We will keep it to 'need to know.' (Figure 1.1).

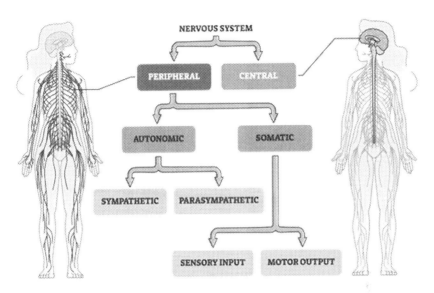

FIGURE 1.1 Divisions of the Nervous System

The Human Nervous System

Our nervous system is divided into two sections: the Central Nervous System (CNS) and the Peripheral Nervous System (PNS). Our CNS includes our brain and spinal cord. The brain contains the amygdala, cerebral cortex, hippocampus, hypothalamus, and pituitary gland, among many other structures. The amygdala, hippocampus, hypothalamus, collectively known as the limbic system and pituitary gland belong to a more primitive region of our fore brain, whereas the human cerebral cortex, the outer layer of the cerebrum, is a more recent evolutionary development. Our PNS consists of the nerves that connect the CNS to the rest of the body (Baum, n.d.). For this book, we will limit it to the adrenal glands, heart, lungs, and muscles.

Our five senses include sight and hearing, as well as our senses of smell, taste, and touch. They all lie within the PNS and are constantly delivering information, which we call stimuli, to our CNS. Within milliseconds, our brain processes the information, paying close attention to potential threats. The CNS relays information back out to the PNS to keep us safe (Visible Body, 2023).

The PNS is further divided into the Autonomic Nervous System (ANS) and the Somatic Nervous System (SNS). The ANS is referred to as involuntary, meaning that you don't direct it through conscious thought. It coordinates the functioning of internal organs like your heart, lungs, and digestive system. For example, your heart beats without you telling it to. The ANS itself is divided into the Sympathetic Nervous System, also known as the 'fight or flight' nervous system, and the Parasympathetic Nervous System, also known as the 'rest and digest' nervous system. Conversely, the SNS is referred to as voluntary because it is directed by conscious thought. It coordinates the functioning of muscles (for example, you consciously wave at a friend who you see waving at you) (National Cancer Institute, 2019).

Sympathetic and Parasympathetic Systems

Cells need oxygen and sugar to make energy. When a sensory stimulus arrives in our brain, our brain assesses the threat level. If a threat is perceived, the Sympathetic Nervous System is activated. Adrenaline and noradrenaline are released from the adrenal glands into the bloodstream. The endocrine system responds to these two hormones, causing the heart and breathing rates to increase, pupils to dilate, blood vessels to muscles to dilate, and sweat glands to contract. These physical changes cause blood, carrying oxygen and sugar, to be directed to cells that need to make energy, specifically cells in the heart, lungs, and muscles. If the threat persists, cortisol is secreted to move sugar, stored in the liver and muscles, to those cells that must make energy to keep us safe (Harvard Health, 2020). Because the body is now primed to fight or flee, it is called the 'fight or flight' nervous system (nugget). The Parasympathetic Nervous System has the opposite effect. Once the threat has passed, our body relaxes. Through what is commonly referred to as a negative feedback loop, secretions of the stress hormones decrease and so the heart and breathing rates slow, the pupils constrict, and sweat glands relax. Our body resumes its normal functions, including replenishing sugar reserves. We can call the Parasympathetic Nervous System the 'rest and digest' nervous system (nugget) (Harvard Health, 2020; McCorry, 2007) (Figure 1.2).

Nervous system

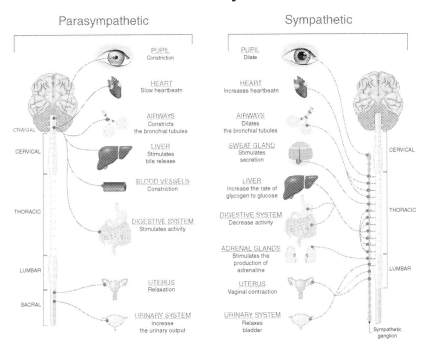

FIGURE 1.2 Effects of the Activation of the Parasympathetic Nervous System versus the Sympathetic Nervous System

You see, some parts of our brain work really well during times of stress, and others do not. The more primitive parts of our brain have served us well for millennia when avoiding predation, at least long enough to reproduce, was our only goal (Stewart, 2020)—that is, when a quick, impulsive reaction was required. However, it does not work so well in class. But thoughtful, well-considered responses take more time. Planning, organizing, decision-making, monitoring, and correcting errors in responses are all the domains of the cerebral cortex, in particular, the prefrontal cortex, the PFC (nugget) (Shapiro, 2021). A common term in the field of education for these actions of the PFC is *executive functioning* (Goldstein et al., n.d.) (Figure 1.3).

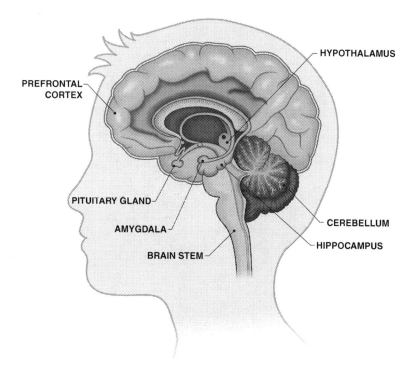

FIGURE 1.3 The Limbic System of the Brain

Break Time #1A! Instead of reading on, take a few minutes and ponder these questions.

- ◆ When did you see Kelly's 'fight or flight' reactive nervous system in control
- ◆ When did you see evidence of her 'rest and digest' nervous system, which allows for executive functioning?
- ◆ Humans can register safety and danger, an ability referred to as 'neuroception.' Where and why did Kelly's neuroception detect a safer environment?

Memories: Regular and Traumatic

We will now look at the important interplay between the nervous system and the endocrine system. Experiences form memories;

some of them are happy, and some we wish we could forget. To understand memories, we need to understand how the limbic system, pituitary gland, and cerebral cortex work together and how these parts of the nervous system interact with the endocrine system. The endocrine system is made of glands, like the adrenal glands, throughout the body which secrete hormones directly into the bloodstream.

A sensory stimulus is received and sent to the amygdala. The amygdala analyzes the stimulus for its threat level. Incidentally, the amygdala registers physical and social threats in the same way (nugget) (Stewart, 2020). In the absence of a threat, the information is then sent to the hippocampus, where it is contextualized for learning, sequenced, and organized. Finally, it is consolidated, that is to say, preserved into a more stable memory and then moved into long-term storage (Tyng et al., 2017). This consolidation happens during sleep, perhaps even several periods of sleep (McGaugh, 2000). The cerebral cortex, in particular the PFC, evolved more recently during human evolution and is where non-traumatic long-term memory storage is located (University of Queensland, n.d.).

Here is an example of a non-stressful or non-traumatic memory: When prompted by your mom during your weekly phone call, you tell her about a surprise birthday party your friend threw for you last weekend. Your story makes sense with a logical beginning, middle, and end, and it will have a fair amount of detail (Wolff, 2017). Hopefully, it is not a memory of a traumatic event. As stated, these memories are stored in your PFC, specifically your neocortex.

But, when recalling a traumatic memory, especially if the person has not been able to sleep, things are very different. When the event first occurred, the amygdala registered a threat, a heightened emotional state. While the intensity of the information was transferred to the hippocampus, the hippocampus's ability to do its job became impaired by activation of the *HPA* axis. The 'H' stands for Hypothalamus, the part of the brain that links the nervous system to the endocrine system. The 'P' stands for Pituitary Gland, which is also located in the brain. The 'A' stands for Adrenal Glands, which are located atop each kidney.

The axis works like this: the *H*ypothalamus sends the message to the *P*ituitary gland, which in turn notifies the *A*drenal glands to start secreting stress hormones, adrenaline, noradrenaline, and then cortisol (Figure 1.4).

When the stress hormones reach the brain, the PFC and hippocampal functions become limited, while the functioning of the amygdala increases (Arnsten, 2009; Government of Canada, 2023). The result of the disconnect between the amygdala and the hippocampus means that a fragmented, emotionally charged memory is created (Stephens & Wand, 2012). Information that was crucial to safety may have been seared into the person's memory, while less crucial details may be hazy or even forgotten. The context and sequence of events were limited because the hippocampal functioning became limited (Cozolino, 2017; Government of Canada, 2023; Wolff, 2017). These memories are stored in parts of the brain associated with non-verbal memories,

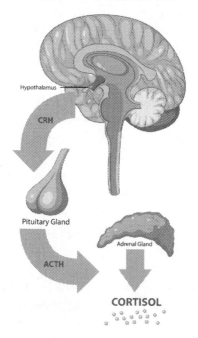

FIGURE 1.4 The Hypothalamic-Pituitary-Adrenal Axis (HPA Axis)

like sights, smells, and sounds (McClelland & Gilyard, 2019). A linear, detailed narrative, like the birthday party, cannot be expected from someone whose amygdala has hijacked their PFC (nugget) (McCook, 2015) (Figure 1.5).

The amygdala is not under voluntary control. Whenever the amygdala registers a sensory stimulus similar to the one registered during the original event, it may send the person right back into those moments. For them, the moment is happening now (Wolff, 2017). And, the trigger could be something as innocuous as an odor, a song playing on the radio, an item of clothing, or an assignment in art class. The PFC is silenced again. It can't say, 'Wait. You're safe!' (nugget).

There is a short but very clear video called *Understanding Trauma: Learning Brain vs Survival Brain*.[1] Hard-copy readers, you can access the video by following these steps:

1. Go to YouTube.
2. Search for *Understanding Trauma, Learning Brain vs. Survival Brain* by Jacob Ham.

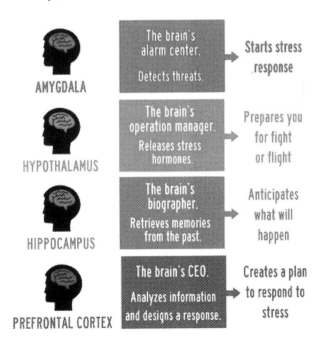

FIGURE 1.5 The Brain's Response to Stress

To be clear, trauma is a dangerous, distressing experience that produces intense physical and psychological stress reactions overwhelming the capacity to cope. It often results in intense emotional and physical reactions, feelings of helplessness, and terror. Its recurrence has lasting physical and mental adverse effects (Fratto, 2016). The American Psychological Association (2015) describes trauma as 'an emotional response to a terrible event'. According to the *Diagnostic and Statistical Manual of Mental Disorders, Fifth Edition* (American Psychiatric Association, 2013), a traumatic event includes exposure to actual or threatened death, serious injury, or sexual violence. The broad definition includes exposure to or experience of an event or series of events that are frightening or threatening and have lasting effects that are overwhelming and challenge one's ability to cope (National Child Traumatic Stress Network [NCTSN], 2014).

Unfortunately, a domino effect can occur whereby stress in one part of someone's life can result in stress in other parts. It's called *stress proliferation* (nugget) (Ward, 2014). For example, someone with one ACE may then have difficulties with employability, which leads to job loss, which leads to homelessness, etc. (Pearlin et al., 1997).

Post-Traumatic Stress Disorder (PTSD)

As part of the body's fight/flight survival response, one feels afraid during and after the traumatic event. However, for some people, whether they were the victim or simply saw or heard about the event, the issue does not resolve within a month and begins impacting daily life. For these people, a diagnosis made by a trained professional is in order (Mayo Foundation for Medical Education and Research, 2022). Pay attention to how PTSD might look for young children.

Symptoms of PTSD
Flashbacks, nightmares, emotional distress to something that is a reminder of the event

Avoiding people, places, and events that are reminders of the
event

Detachment, numbness, feelings of hopelessness, negative
thoughts about self, others, or the world

Easily startled, feeling 'on guard' all the time, self-destructive
behaviors, shame, guilt, aggressive outbursts, difficulty sleep-
ing, difficulty concentrating

The onset of PTSD symptoms varies greatly from person to
person. Further, it can last for weeks, months, or years without
treatment and impacts daily functioning. Children, especially
if 6 years of age and under, may also experience the following:
wetting the bed, either choosing not to speak or being unable to
speak, needing to be with a parent or caregiver (clingy), reenact-
ing the trauma in play, frightening dreams that may or may not
be of the actual event (Mayo Foundation for Medical Education
and Research, 2022; National Institute of Mental Health, 2023).

Fight, Flight, Freeze, and Fawn (FFFFs)

As stated, whether the amygdala senses an actual stressor or a
stimulus that is evocative of a past stressor, an uncontrollable
physiological response will be the result (Doyle, 2023; Guy-
Evans, 2023). We are going to dive a bit deeper into the fight/
flight response, contrast it to the freeze response, and add in Pete
Walker's fawn response. Whatever the response, optimizing
safety is the goal (Mobbs et al., 2015).

Fight/Flight

You can easily spy indications of a student in fight/flight mode
due to their rapid, shallow breathing, pounding heart, sweat-
ing, pupil dilation, or tightened jaw. Depending on the student
and their age, perhaps you will also see behaviors like stomp-
ing, crying, or acting out violently. If the student has access to
the door, they may be fidgety and restless. You may see their
eyes darting to and fro before they flee the area (Doyle, 2023).

That newly created energy has to be used for something. Evolutionarily speaking, avoiding a fight altogether by accessing an escape route increases the chances of survival (Guy-Evans, 2023).

Freeze

A student in a freeze may appear to have zoned out. You may think 'in one ear, out the other' as you try to interact. Such a student may also appear stiff, with a pounding heart. A freeze may be total or partial. Symptoms can range from total dissociation to a temporary inability to verbalize or move (Lyon, 2016). If this interests you, you may want to research Stephen Porges' Polyvagal Theory.

Fawn

The fawn response might be entirely new to you. A child with a narcissistic, abusive parent may have found out that fighting and fleeing only make the inevitable punishment far worse. Fawning may be the only option left available. Fawning is losing oneself, dropping all personal boundaries, and surrendering all personal needs to serve the parent's needs. Such children serve the parents as housekeepers, cooks, punching bags, or even sexual partners. Neglected children may also develop the fawn response. It is considered to be a response to both sympathetic and parasympathetic activation (Doyle, 2023; Walker, 2003).

These adaptations for survival become maladaptive behaviors outside of the survival context; thus, they will have far-reaching consequences later in life. Simply recognizing these behaviors in your students is the first step in mitigating them (nugget) (Figure 1.6).

Break Time #1B! Instead of reading on, watch the following video on YouTube and answer the questions.

The video is called *Trauma and the Incredible Hulk*.[2] Hard-copy readers, follow these steps:

1. Go to YouTube.
2. Search *Trauma and the Incredible Hulk* by Jacob Ham.

- ◆ Why are restrictions and consequences counterproductive to your *hulked-out* student?
- ◆ When a student is beginning to *hulk out*, what is the best strategy to employ?
- ◆ What can you do once a student has *hulked out*?
- ◆ How does the student feel after the *hulk-out* has subsided?
- ◆ How can your classroom or school better support students who have *hulked out*?

Compare and contrast the two graphs. Do you see how the curve is flatter and the time for recovery is quicker in Figure 1.7 when appropriate Cognitive-Behavioral Therapy (CBT) strategies are applied? How to apply CBT will be discussed in Chapter 5.

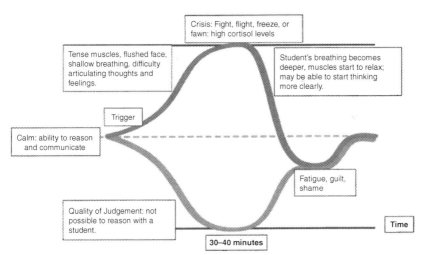

Based on the work of Lee Allan Rengert and Paul Smith (1986)

Levels of Cortisol and Quality of Judgement during Emotional Dysregulation

Red Curve- cortisol levels may increase to a "crisis level" after the stress-response is triggered

Yellow Curve- ability to reason and problem-solve very low

FIGURE 1.6 Increase of Cortisol and Adrenaline Levels Following a Stress Trigger

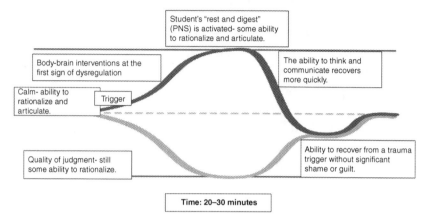

Body-Brain interventions after a trigger/signs of emotional dysregulation

Red Curve:cortisol levels do not reach "crisis level" after a stress response is triggered.

Yellow Curve: the ability to rationalize and problem solve is compromised but recovers relatively quickly.

FIGURE 1.7 Increase of Cortisol and Adrenaline When Body-Brain Interventions Are Engaged Following a Trigger

Chronic Stress and Changes to the Brain

Exposure to ACEs is shown to have long-lasting effects not just on the physical and mental health of young people but also on the structure and functioning of their brains and, of course, their academic success (Arnsten, 2009; McEwen et al., 2016).

Epigenetics

Let's start with epigenetics, which we will be returning to in Chapter 2. Every cell in the body contains the same genes. As cells specialize to do a particular job, some proteins are not needed, and thus the genes that create them are turned off while other proteins are required, and so the genes that make them are turned on. For example, insulin is a protein that is made in the beta cells of the pancreas. In all other cells, that gene has been turned off. Epigenetic modifications do happen naturally during and over a lifetime, but they can also be induced (Jiang et al., 2019). Turning genes off can be accomplished in several ways, but we will address one way called gene methylation, which simply means that a methyl group, CH_3, is added to a gene. Conversely, demethlylation turns genes on. Exposure to ACEs causes certain genes related to self-regulation and the HPA axis to turn off (Jiang et al., 2019).

Brain Connections

Research shows that neural connections between the hippocampus and PFC are weaker in children who have been exposed to ACEs. In girls, there are also fewer connections between the amygdala and PFC. This double whammy means that female students are more likely to develop mood disorders like anxiety and depression (Burghy et al., 2012; Nakazawa, 2016; Starr, 2020).

Exposure to Stress Hormones

Chronic exposure to noradrenaline correlates with less gray matter in the PFC, which results in a greater reliance on the hardwired and more primitive emotional neural circuitry and greater deficits in PFC functioning, like regulation of behaviors and impairments in working memory (Arnsten, 2009). Reduced self-control means a higher likelihood of developing addictions to drugs and alcohol (Patock-Peckham et al., 2020). Another vicious cycle is created. Many mental health disorders are linked to the amygdala, such as panic disorder, mood disorders, PTSD, and Intermittent Explosive Disorder (Cleveland Clinic, 2023). Research shows that, like the PFC, hippocampal volume is also reduced in children suffering from ACEs (Teicher et al., 2012). High blood pressure from overexposure to adrenaline is linked to heart attack and stroke. Cortisol exposure over the long term is linked to obesity and diabetes because it encourages overeating to replenish glucose reserves (Harvard Health, 2020; van der Valk et al., 2018). Additionally, deficits in cognition, including memory retrieval, may be seen in elderly patients who have experienced a lifetime of overexposure to cortisol (McEwen et al., 2016; Souza-Talarico et al., 2011).

War

Before we move to the next chapter, let's discuss war and refugees. According to the United Nations High Commissioner for Refugees, there were 35.3 million refugees at the end of 2022, with the majority coming from Syria, Ukraine, and Afghanistan (*Global Trends Report*, 2022). You may find yourself with refugee children in your school. These children have seen family, friends, neighbors, and pets injured or killed. They have watched their homes, schools, and neighborhoods reduced to rubble. It is sometimes difficult for agencies to deliver food and medicine to these areas, further creating a sense of despair. Their sense of safety has been totally destroyed. If these children cannot verbally express how they feel, their behaviors might. What might chronic stress look like in your classroom? It might look like withdrawing, aggressiveness, or difficulties in speaking, breathing, and moving Save the Children International, 2023). For such children, loving and caring parents/caregivers are more important than ever (nugget) (Farajallah et al., 2022). We will address this in greater detail in Chapter 3.

As society makes its way through the Fourth Industrial Revolution, skills associated with the PFC, like rationalizing, predicting, complex problem-solving, and collaborating, will be in greater demand (Arnsten, 2009; Heriot-Watt University, 2022). We cannot understate the impact that ACEs have on our students' lives, nor can we understate the need for a large repertoire of intervention strategies. The good news is that there are evidence-based interventions that will help you to help your students, like Kelly, to mitigate the damage done by ACEs. Keep reading!

Answers to Brain Breaks

Break Time #1A! Instead of reading on, take a few minutes and ponder these questions.

a. When did you see Kelly's 'Fight or Flight' reactive nervous system in control?
In Ms. Simpson's class, specifically when doing the assignment about a family Thanksgiving. Ms. Simpson escalated the situation by threatening to call home. This prompted Kelly to flee the room.
b. When did you see evidence of her 'Rest and Digest' nervous system, which allows for executive functioning?
In Mrs. Jackson's class when Mrs. Jackson soothingly spoke to her and reassured her everything was going to be okay. Finally, Mrs. Jackson gave Kelly the time and space to self-regulate, preventing Kelly from leaving the building.

c. Humans can register safety and danger, an ability referred to as 'neuroception.' Where and why did Kelly's neuroception detect a safer environment?
Mrs. Jackson's room was deemed by Kelly to be safer. Mrs. Jackson was calming, not threatening. Kelly was given a suitable option whereby she could calm down in sight of an adult.

Break Time #1B! Instead of reading on, watch the following video on YouTube and answer the questions.

a. Why are restrictions and consequences counterproductive to your *hulked-out* student?
It makes the situation far worse. They become more dysregulated and perhaps more violent to protect themselves.
b. When a student is beginning to *hulk out*, what is the best strategy to employ?
To prevent further escalation, the student can be reminded of the things that they love and care about most. Also, the student can use 'body-brain' emotional regulation strategies to engage their 'rest and digest' nervous system. *This is explained in Chapter 5.*
c. What can you do once a student has *hulked out*?
There isn't much you can do other than keep everyone safe. The student needs time to metabolize the cortisol and adrenaline in their system.
d. How does the student feel after the *hulk-out* has subsided?
The student may experience feelings of guilt and may feel exhausted.
e. How can your classroom or school better support students who have *hulked out*?
Providing chill-out spaces within the classroom or the school in which the student can have time and space to metabolize the stress hormones.

Notes

1 https://www.youtube.com/watch?app=desktop&v=KoqaUANGvpA.
2 https://www.youtube.com/watch?v=o0FtfB4Co0k.

References

American Psychiatric Association. (2013). *Diagnostic and statistical manual of mental disorders* (5th ed.). https://doi.org/10.1176/appi.books.9780890425596

American Psychological Association. (2015). *Trauma*. American Psychological Association. https://www.apa.org/topics/trauma#:~:text=Trauma%20is%20an%20emotional%20response,symptoms%20like%20headaches%20or%20nausea

Arnsten, A. F. T. (2009, June). Stress signalling pathways that impair prefrontal cortex structure and function. *Nature Reviews. Neuroscience.* https://www.ncbi.nlm.nih.gov/pmc/articles/PMC2907136/?ref=anangsha.me

Baum, H. (n.d.). *The nervous system*. University of Cincinnati. https://www.uc.edu/content/dam/uc/ce/images/OLLI/Page%20Content/The%20Nervous%20System.pdf

Burghy, C. A., Stodola, D. E., Ruttle, P. L., Molloy, E. K., Armstrong, J. M., Oler, J. A., Fox, M. E., Hayes, A. S., Kalin, N. H., Essex, M. J., Davidson, R. J., & Birn, R. M. (2012). Developmental pathways to amygdala-prefrontal function and internalizing symptoms in adolescence. *Nature Neuroscience, 15*(12), 1736–1741. https://doi.org/10.1038/nn.3257

Cleveland Clinic. (2023, April 11). *The amygdala: A small part of your brain's biggest abilities*. https://my.clevelandclinic.org/health/body/24894-amygdala

Cozolino, L. (2017). *The Neuroscience of psychotherapy: Healing the social brain* (3rd ed.). W. W. Norton & Co.

de Souza-Talarico, J. N., Marin, M. F., Sindi, S., & Lupien, S. J. (2011). Effects of stress hormones on the brain and cognition: Evidence from normal to pathological aging. *Dementia & Neuropsychologia, 5*(1), 8–16. https://doi.org/10.1590/S1980-57642011DN05010003

Doyle, K. (2023, August 16). *Fight, flight, freeze, fawn: Our natural response to threats*. Mountainside. https://mountainside.com/blog/mental-health/fight-flight-freeze-fawn-our-natural-response-to-threats/

Farajallah, I., Reda, O., Moffic, H. S., Peteet, J. R., & Hankir, A. (2022, March 8). *The psychosocial impacts of war and armed conflict on children*. Psychiatric Times. https://www.psychiatrictimes.com/view/the-psychosocial-impacts-of-war-and-armed-conflict-on-children

Fratto, C. M. (2016). Trauma-informed care for youth in foster care. *Archives of Psychiatric Nursing, 30*(3), 439–446. https://doi.org/10.1016/j.apnu.2016.01.007

Goldstein, S., Naglieri, J. A., Princiotta, D., & Otero, T. M. (n.d.). *Articles. –* Dr Sam Goldstein. https://samgoldstein.com/resources/articles/general/a-history-of-executive-functioning-as-a-theoretical-and-clinical-construct.aspx

Government of Canada, D. of J. (2023, January 20). *The Impact of Trauma on Adult Sexual Assault Victims*. PART III – How Trauma Affects Memory and Recall. https://www.justice.gc.ca/eng/rp-pr/jr/trauma/p4.html#:~:text=Stress%20and%20fear%20heighten%20activation,in%20episodic%20or%20explicit%20memory

Guy-Evans, O. (2023, November 9). *Fight, flight, freeze, or fawn: How we respond to threats*. Simply Psychology. https://www.simplypsychology.org/fight-flight-freeze-fawn.html

Harvard Health. (2020, July 6). *Understanding the stress response*. https://www.health.harvard.edu/staying-healthy/understanding-the-stress-response?gad_source=1&gclid=CjwKCAiA44OtBhAOEiwAj4gpOck9Uir4wuq-4Z5qTLux-wbhwG5abH--5wsECRPL30208UqSyYeeihoCkcwQAvD_BwE

Heriot-Watt University. (2022, September 2). *Preparing for the fourth industrial revolution: Top skills and careers*. https://www.hw.ac.uk/news/articles/2022/preparing-for-the-fourth-industrial.htm

Jiang, S., Postovit, L., Cattaneo, A., Binder, E. B., & Aitchison, K. J. (2019, October 11). *Epigenetic modifications in stress response genes associated with childhood trauma*. Frontiers. https://www.frontiersin.org/articles/10.3389/fpsyt.2019.00808/full

Lyon, B. (2016, January 12). *Anatomy of a freeze – Or dorsal vagal shut-down*. Center for Healing Shame. https://healingshame.com/articles/anatomy-of-a-freeze-or-dorsal-vagal-shutdown-bret-lyon-phd#:~:text=However%2C%20when%20the%20sympathetic%20system,a%20much%20more%20recent%20addition

Mayo Foundation for Medical Education and Research. (2022, December 13). *Post-traumatic stress disorder (PTSD)*. Mayo Clinic. https://www.mayoclinic.org/diseases-conditions/post-traumatic-stress-disorder/symptoms-causes/syc-20355967

McClelland, D., & Gilyard, C., (2019, August 27). *Trauma and the brain*. Phoenix Society for Burn Survivors. Retrieved January 12, 2024, from https://www.phoenix-society.org/resources/calming-trauma

McCook, A. (2015, July 15). *PTSD sufferers store memories in a different part of the brain*. PTSD Association of Canada. Retrieved January 12, 2024, from https://www.ptsdassociation.com/ptsd-sufferers/2015/7/15/ptsd-sufferers-store-memories-in-different-part-of-brain

McCorry, L. K. (2007). Physiology of the autonomic nervous system. *American Journal of Pharmaceutical Education, 71*(4), 78. https://doi.org/10.5688/aj710478

McEwen, B., Nasca, C., & Gray, J. (2016, January). Stress effects on neuronal structure: Hippocampus, amygdala, and prefrontal cortex. *Neuropsychopharmacology: Official Publication of the American College of Neuropsychopharmacology*. https://pubmed.ncbi.nlm.nih.gov/26076834/

McGaugh, J. L. (2000). Memory – A century of consolidation. *Science (New York, N.Y.), 287*(5451), 248–251. https://doi.org/10.1126/science.287.5451.24

Mobbs, D., Hagan, C. C., Dalgleish, T., Silston, B., & Prévost, C. (2015, February 7). *The ecology of human fear: Survival optimization and the nervous system*. Frontiers. https://www.frontiersin.org/articles/10.3389/fnins.2015.00055/full

Nakazawa, D. J. (2016, September 15). *7 ways childhood adversity changes a child's brain*. ACEs Too High. https://acestoohigh.com/2016/09/08/7-ways-childhood-adversity-changes-a-childs-brain/

National Cancer Institute. (2019). *Introduction to the nervous system*. Cancer.gov. https://training.seer.cancer.gov/anatomy/nervous/

National Child Traumatic Stress Network. (2014). *Trauma types*. www.nctsn.org/what-is-child-trauma/trauma-types

National Institute of Mental Health. (2023). *Post-traumatic stress disorder*. National Institute of Mental Health. https://www.nimh.nih.gov/health/topics/post-traumatic-stress-disorder-ptsd

Patock-Peckham, J. A., Belton, D. A., D'Ardenne, K., Tein, J., Bauman, D. C., Infurna, F. J., Sanabria, F., Curtis, J., Morgan-Lopez, A. A., & McClure, S. M. (2020). Dimensions of childhood trauma and their direct and indirect links to PTSD, impaired control over drinking, and alcohol-related-problems. *Addictive Behaviors Reports, 12*, 100304. https://doi.org/10.1016/j.abrep.2020.100304

Pearlin, L. I., Aneshensel, C. S., & Leblanc, A. J. (1997). The forms and mechanisms of stress proliferation: The case of AIDS caregivers. *Journal of Health and Social Behavior, 38*(3), 223–236. https://doi.org/10.2307/2955368

Save the Children International. (2023, January 30). *Surviving is just the beginning: The impact of conflict on children's Mental Health*. https://www.savethechildren.net/blog/surviving-just-beginning-impact-conflict-children-s-mental-health#:~:text=Anxiety%2C%20Loneliness%20and%20Insecurity,anxiety%20in%20war%2Daffected%20children

Shapiro, J. (2021, November 5). *Two parts of the brain govern much of mental life*. Psychology Today. https://www.psychologytoday.com/ca/blog/thinking-in-black-white-and-gray/202111/two-parts-the-brain-govern-much-mental-life

Starr, A. (2020, January 4). *How aces affect the brain*. Different Brains. https://differentbrains.org/how-aces-affect-the-brain/

Stephens, M. A. C., & Wand, G. (2012). Stress and the HPA axis: Role of glucocorticoids in alcohol dependence. *Alcohol Research: Current Reviews*. https://www.ncbi.nlm.nih.gov/pmc/articles/PMC3860380/

Stewart, P. (2020, May 11). *Fight, flight, freeze: Our brains on feedback*. Https://www.Forbes.com/Sites/Forbescoachescouncil/2022/05/11/Fight-Flight-Freeze-Our-Brains-On-Feedback/?sh=58f62760868e. Retrieved January 12, 2024, from https://www.phoenix-society.org/resources/calming-trauma

Teicher, M. H., Anderson, C. M., & Polcari, A. (2012). Childhood maltreatment is associated with reduced volume in the hippocampal subfields CA3, dentate gyrus, and subiculum. *Proceedings of the National Academy of Sciences, 109*(9), E563–E572. https://doi.org/10.1073/pnas.1115396109

Tyng, C. M., Amin, H. U., Saad, M. N., & Malik, A. S. (2017, August 24). *The influences on emotion and memory. Frontiers in Psychology.* Retrieved January 12, 2024, from https://www.ncbi.nlm.nih.gov/pmc/articles/PMC5573739/

UNHCR. (2022). *Global Trends Report 2022.* https://www.unhcr.org/global-trends-report-2022

University of Queensland. (n.d.). *Where are memories stored in the brain?* Queensland Brain Institute. Retrieved January 12, 2024, from https://qbi.uq.edu.au/brain-basics/memory/where-are-memories-stored

van der Valk, E. S., Savas, M., & van Rossum, E. F. C. (2018, June). *Stress and obesity: Are there more susceptible individuals?* Current Obesity Reports. https://www.ncbi.nlm.nih.gov/pmc/articles/PMC5958156/

Visible Body Learn Anatomy. (2023). *The Five Senses.* https://www.visiblebody.com/learn/nervous/five-senses#:~:text=Nerves%20relay%20the%20signals%20to,and%20touch%20(tactile%20perception)

Walker, Pete. (2003, January/February). *Codependency, trauma and the fawn response.* M.A. Psychotherapy. https://www.pete-walker.com/codependencyFawnResponse.htm

Ward, B. (2014, February 21). *Stress proliferation.* Wiley Online Library. https://onlinelibrary.wiley.com/doi/abs/10.1002/9781118410868.wbehibs108

Wolff, B. (2017, November 19). *The difference between normal memories and traumatic memories: Addiction counselling.* Addiction Counselling. https://www.torontoaddictioncounselling.com/the-difference-between-normal-memories-and-traumatic-memories/

2

Intergenerational Trauma

In a social setting a few years ago, I met a teacher who spent one year working in a small Indigenous community in the Canadian North. My first question was, 'How did you like it?' She said it was confusing and frustrating. As I listened, she explained her frustration trying to teach students who 'rarely' came to school. I responded with, 'I wonder if the residential school legacy is a factor?' She explained that was the confusing part for her because none of the children she taught went to residential schools, nor did many of their parents. She felt there was no reason for them not to attend school (by author Dr. Lori Brown, personal communication, 2023).

As educators, we need to understand that the effects of trauma can be passed to future generations via a variety of mechanisms, some better understood than others. Technically, *intergenerational* trauma refers to trauma passed from exposed parent to children, and *transgenerational* trauma refers to trauma passed from exposed parent to children, grandchildren, great-grandchildren, etc. (nugget) (American Psychological Association, 2023). We will focus on the different ways in which trauma may have been passed on to your students, as opposed to how many generations removed they are from the original trauma. For you, the issue is the students in front of you now.

DOI: 10.4324/9781032707945-4

Back to ACEs

The original pyramid that we showed you in the introduction has recently been amended as shown in Figure 2.1.

Before reading further, take a moment and compare Figure 0.1 to Figure 2.1. What is new? If you answered something like, 'Two tiers have been added to the bottom, which extends exposure to ACEs past the household, into the community, and across generations,' you are correct (nugget).

Prenatal

Maternal stress, depression, anxiety, and smoking are just a few of the factors that can result in prenatal programming. Prenatal programming is the manifestation of conditions in the fetus due

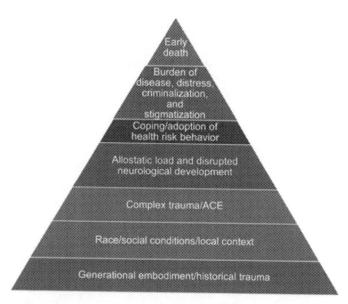

FIGURE 2.1 The ACE Pyramid

Source: Centers for Disease Control and Prevention (2014). Violence Prevention: *The ACE Pyramid* (adapted by RYSE Youth Center)

to factors that occur *in utero* at times that are particularly sensitive to development (Kwon & Kim, 2017).

Epigenetics

We will begin with evidence pointing to the epigenetic transmission of trauma. Remember, prolonged exposure to stress results in the secretion of cortisol, which keeps the body revved up by releasing stored sugar into the bloodstream. Sugar is a necessary ingredient in creating energy for the fight/flight response. In Chapter 1, we stated that trauma can cause genes related to the HPA axis to be turned off via methylation and on via demethylation. Recent studies show that children who had not been exposed to trauma may have altered DNA methylations if their parents had been exposed. For example, adult children of Holocaust survivors showed higher rates of anxiety and even PTSD, even though they had not experienced trauma in their own lives. Further, those with PTSD had low cortisol levels (Yehuda & Lehrner, 2018). Low cortisol levels were also seen in pregnant women who, on September 11, 2001, were working in or near the World Trade Center and who then developed PTSD. The results were more pronounced if the women were in their third trimesters when they had to flee the area. They typically delivered smaller babies with lower cortisol levels than those who did not develop PTSD. The infants were reexamined about one year later, and cortisol levels were still low. Their PTSD mothers reported that their babies were difficult to soothe and more fearful (Yehuda, 2022). Perhaps you are thinking that is a bit of a paradox. If mothers are traumatized, shouldn't their cortisol levels be high?

I also mentioned the term *negative feedback loop* in Chapter 1. Let's recap the negative feedback loop. Stress activates the HPA axis, resulting in increased adrenaline, noradrenaline, and cortisol levels. This primes the body for fight or flight. But, prolonged exposure to cortisol is toxic to the body and brain. To reset hormone levels and to return the body to homeostasis, cortisol acts on the hypothalamus to reduce the production of all three stress hormones (Stephens & Wand, 2012). Cortisol must bind to molecules called receptors to work (Thau et al., 2023). Reduced methylation of the gene NR3C1 that makes the receptor leads to more receptors being made. More receptors and greater sensitivity of the receptors mean lower cortisol levels can have a wildly greater impact. It is posited that really low levels of cortisol are unable to shut down future HPA activity occurring in subsequent traumas. In other words, low cortisol levels seem to convey increased susceptibility to PTSD. And yes, lower methylation of the NR3C1 gene was seen in both mothers who had survived the Holocaust and their children (Yehuda, 2022). The point here is that alterations to the HPA axis are seen in children who were not exposed to the original stressor (nugget).

Interestingly, the children of the fathers who had survived the Holocaust showed greater methylation of the gene (Yehuda, 2022). This study and others indicate that the sex of the parent exposed is also a factor and is likely due to differences in the time of life when egg and sperm are produced (Faulk & Dolinoy, 2011; Yehuda & Lehrner, 2018). Yet people with severe mental health diagnoses other than PTSD have higher than normal cortisol levels (Dziurkowska & Wesolowski, 2021).

The Dutch Famine is a particularly well-documented example of epigenetics across generations. During this famine of 1944–1945, an estimated 20,000 people died of starvation (deBruin, 2020). Studies have shown that male offspring of women who became pregnant during that time showed greater vulnerability later in life to health issues such as diabetes and obesity. In these offspring, there was lower methylation of a gene, IGF2 that creates a growth hormone. This protein regulates growth and development, so lower methylation leads to increased gene expression, which in turn leads to increased production of growth hormone (Painter et al., 2008). That's not a bad thing if the intent is to convey to the fetus information about the environment into which it will be born. But if that environment no longer exists, then perhaps it conveys a vulnerability instead. The children of those males were also heavier in later years. However, offspring of mothers who were born to famine survivors were heavier at birth (De Rooij et al., 2021; Heijmans et al., 2008).

As stated, cortisol is toxic to the brain and body, especially to the developing fetus's brain and body (Coussons-Read, 2013). There is an enzyme that converts cortisol into its inactive form, cortisone. The enzyme is called 11β-HSD2. In otherwise healthy pregnancies, there is a lot of this enzyme in the placenta, suggesting demethylation of its gene. We know that anxiety increases cortisol levels. Yet, studies show downregulation of 11β-HSD2 in the placenta of anxiety-ridden mothers, resulting in more toxic cortisol reaching the fetus (O'Donnell et al., 2012). There are several theories as to why this occurs.

FASD
We will now look at several other factors that affect fetal development. We know that adults turn to alcohol and drugs to relieve life's stressors. We also know that they both negatively impact fetal development because they pass through the placenta. For example, babies born with Fetal Alcohol Spectrum Disorder (FASD) show a wide range of problems that affect their ability to learn and remember but also their ability to control their behaviors, all of which present problems for their teachers. Additionally, such children show greater susceptibility to anxiety and depression (Hellemans et al., 2010). A survey conducted in Canada of elementary students aged 7–9 indicated a prevalence of FASD of 2%–3%, which is similar to estimates of 2%–5% in the USA (Popova, 2018). In 2013, it was estimated that the cost of FASD to the Canadian taxpayer was $1.8 billion (Popova et al., 2015). Sadly, FASD is both prevalent and, for the most part, a preventable illness. Perhaps you are wondering about FASD in your classroom. The printable information sheet called 'Basic Facts about FASDs'[1] from the CDC provides a lot of information. Hard-copy readers, simply follow these steps:

Step 1: Search Centers for Disease Control and Prevention (www.cdc.gov).
Step 2: Once at www.cdc.gov, type in the search box FASD.
Step 3: The link 'Basic Facts about FASD' is the one you want.

Cigarettes
Although not specifically labeled an ACE, cigarette smoking during pregnancy can result in harm to the fetus, which may have lifelong implications (Centers for Disease Control and Prevention, 2014; Ernst et al., 2001). Cigarettes contain thousands of chemicals, including nicotine. Nicotine is an addictive

stimulant (Rogers, 2009). Reduced blood flow to the placenta means less food and oxygen reaching the fetus. Nicotine receptors are already in place in the fetal brain early in development (Dwyer et al., 2009). *In utero* exposure may result in aberrations in fetal neurodevelopment and may lead to a higher risk for substance abuse later in life (Rogers, 2009).

Many studies have shown that prenatal exposure to cigarettes may result in lower birth weight (Gunther et al., 2021). Infants with low birth weight, in particular very low birth weight, are at increased risk of behavioral and intellectual issues, resulting in a greater need for specialized education plans (Di et al., 2022; Horwood et al., 1999).

Maternal Nutrition

In utero nutrition is also important for healthy fetal development. Adequate amounts of calcium, iron, and iodine, as well as vitamins A, C, B6, B12, D, folic acid, protein, and good fats are required for optimal development of the fetus, particularly neurodevelopment (Cortés-Albornoz et al., 2021). The following ACEs may impact the diet of a pregnant woman: war, poverty, depression, lack of education, and gender inequalities, to name a few.

Postnatal

Suppose you have students who have asthma or other respiratory problems, earaches, tooth decay, or developmental delays. It may be because they are exposed to secondhand smoke (Centers for Disease Control and Prevention, 2022). In case any of your students are exposed to secondhand smoke, there is a comprehensive, user-friendly guide about smoking that you can have available to parents called 'Let's Make the Next Generation Tobacco-Free.'[2] For you hard-copy readers, follow these steps:

Step 1: Type in 'www.hhs.gov.'

Step 2: In the search bar, type in 'Let's Make the Next Generation Tobacco-Free.'

Step 3: Scroll down until you see the pdf called '50th Anniversary Surgeon General's Report.'

We will revisit this issue later in the chapter. In reference to the FFFF trauma responses first mentioned in Chapter 1, we wrote, 'These adaptations for survival become maladaptive behaviors outside of the survival context; thus, they will have far-reaching consequences later in life.' Well, now it's later in life, and these ACE-exposed children have children of their own.

Attachment Theory

We will begin by looking at *Attachment Theory* (Bretherton, 1992). It makes sense, from an evolutionary point of view, that attachment to a parent promotes chances for survival in the offspring. From a psychosocial point of view, it is also about the attachment between caregiver and child, and how that attachment can influence other relationships as the child grows up. A child who is comforted, protected, and soothed by a responsive caregiver grows up to be more secure in themselves, more self-reliant, and has a greater self-concept. However, shortcomings in this first, all-important attachment can have negative consequences for any future attachments. Limited opportunities to bond and/or poor-quality bonding may negatively impact a child's sense of safety and security. John Bowlby was the first to describe Attachment Theory. His work was expanded by Mary Ainsworth, who described three styles of attachment (Ackerman, 2023; Cherry, 2023).

1. **Secure attachment** is demonstrated by a child who, while distressed to varying degrees at the separation from the caregiver, knows that the caregiver will return. The child seeks and receives soothing and comfort from the caregiver when upset and thus soon settles down. This is the most common form of attachment.

2. **Avoidant attachment** is demonstrated by a child who does not seem overly distressed by separation from the caregiver and seems to snub the caregiver upon her/his return. This child has a neglectful caregiver or has an abusive caregiver and perhaps has been previously punished for relying on the caregiver and now avoids him/her (Fraley, 2010).

3. **Ambivalent attachment** is a rarer form of attachment, seen in 7%–15% of children in the United States. A child is

very distressed when separated from the caregiver, who is not available to the child as needed, and thus the child learns that they cannot depend on the caregiver. When the caregiver returns, the child has difficulty settling down.

4. **Disorganized attachment** was the last to be added. A child who, although distressed, avoids or resists the parent. The caregiver may elicit feelings of comfort or fear in the child. Thus, the child's behavior toward the caregiver is confused, as they do not know what kind of response they will receive (Kennedy & Kennedy, 2004) (nugget).

Trauma at a young age may result in Oppositional Defiant Disorder, Conduct Disorder, or Post-Traumatic Stress Disorder (Evans et al., 2008; Gershoff, 2002; Milot et al., 2010). Such children may show issues related to attachment. Furthermore, attachment disorders may emerge in childhood, such as Reactive Attachment Disorder, which affects the ability to manage emotions, and Disinhibited Social Engagement Disorder, which results in behaviors toward strangers that lack social boundaries (Seim et al., 2022).

Given the new expanded ACE list from the beginning of this chapter, we are going to play a game; actually, it's a brain break that we call 'Count the ACEs.' As you read the rest of this chapter, count the exposures to ACEs that can occur across generations in the groups we discuss.

Historic Trauma

Trauma perpetuated against an individual can be passed on to that individual's descendants. Additionally, trauma perpetrated against a particular community can have lasting and cumulative effects on its future generations; we will call it *historical trauma*.

Historical trauma is cumulative emotional and psychological wounding over the lifespan and across generations, emanating from massive group trauma experiences.

(Brave Heart, 2003)

Specifically, we will look at colonialism and associated racism in communities in Canada. However, there are many examples around the world where colonized Indigenous groups have experienced similar treatment, including the United States, Australia, and New Zealand (Maple-Brown & Hampton, 2020). Regardless of the country, the Indigenous Peoples were left with a legacy of trauma that resulted in addictions and vast socio-economic disparities (Smallwood et al., 2020) (nugget). The following examples are discussed mainly as psychosocial factors, but this does not imply that epigenetic and/or other biological factors are not also at play. Read that last sentence again.

Reserves

Behavior can be learned through social interactions and reinforcement (Bandura, 1977; McLeod, 2023). Some survivors of colonialism experienced trauma that they then passed on to the next generation. Just before the establishment of the residential school system was the establishment of reserves. Around 1830, Indigenous Peoples were forcibly removed from their productive lands as colonists dictated. In contrast to their homeland, the reserves they were moved to were small and relatively barren. The creation of reserves was particularly jarring in light of how deeply meaningful the homeland is to Indigenous Peoples. The government was able to do this under what became known as the Indian Act of 1857 (Coates, 2008; Josewski et al., 2023; Milloy, 2008).

Indigenous people, though deeply heterogeneous and greatly varied, are in and of place, anchored in a connection to homelands, even if separated from those homelands upon which their kinship and genealogical being stretch back beyond time itself. Associated with this groundedness of Indigeneity is an undeniable truth that many Indigenous people have asserted, namely, that they have an orientation to the world that is fundamentally rooted in land, water, and ecologies.

(Josewski et al., 2023)

Residential Schools

Nicholas Flood Davin, a Canadian politician and journalist, had been dispatched to the United States and western Canada to study the industrial boarding schools. In his report to the Canadian government, he felt that the US boarding school model was an effective way to eradicate the heritage of the students (Davin, 1879).

During a 150-year period, from the 1880s to the 1990s, over 150,000 First Nations, Inuit, and Metis Nation children were forcibly removed from their homes, their parents, and their communities to attend the 139 residential schools (NCTR, 2021; NCTR, 2023). The intent was to assimilate them into the Eurocentric, white, Christian society of the colonists, and to make this happen, they separated the children from their heritage so that their language and culture died off (Agular & Halseth, 2015).

The schools were set up and funded, or underfunded, by the Canadian government, but the running of the schools was outsourced to the Anglican, Methodist, Presbyterian, and United churches, and 60% being run by the Catholic Church, with no consequences for the abhorrent treatment some of the residential schools' missionaries meted out (Miller, 2024; RCAP, 1996; National Center for Truth and Reconciliation, 2021). In some instances, children, even younger than your kindergarten students, were severely punished, tortured in fact, for acknowledging their own culture, or language in any way; in other words, government-sanctioned cultural genocide (The Royal Commission on Aboriginal Peoples, 1996). They suffered horrific physical, sexual, and psychological abuse. Their symbolic long hair was cut short, and they were given a Eurocentric name or merely a number (Hanson et al., 2020). They couldn't even communicate with siblings in their own language (Union of Ontario Indians, 2013). They were malnourished, exposed to the elements, and knowingly exposed to tuberculosis, influenza, smallpox, and whooping cough, to name a few (RCAP, 1996). Compromised immune systems and severe abuse meant thousands of these children did not return home. Others were sent home to die (Hanson and Cherkowski, 2024; Department of Justice Canada, n.d.).

Those who did return home had been deprived of respectful parent role models, as well as nurturing, loving families (National Council for Truth and Reconciliation, 2021). They were also deprived of a proper education because part of their day was spent in forced manual labor to keep the school running as cheaply as possible (Miller, 2024) (nugget).

At the age of 16 or 17, the children left residential school. It is of no surprise that they had difficulty integrating into white society, as they had little education or valuable vocational training, and they were still viewed with a racial bias. Spending their childhood at these schools meant missing out on their ancestors' wisdom, history, and experiences as told by the storytellers in their communities. Without their language or ancestral knowledge and experiences, they had difficulty reintegrating into their own communities (Ferguson, 2023). Some stated that they belonged in neither world (Menzies, 2024). The residential school experience set the stage, via stress proliferation, for poverty and maladaptive coping strategies, which then oozed into their communities (Bombay et al., 2014). Inequities grew as these 'graduates' had children of their own. *Intergenerational stress proliferation* was the result (nugget).

High rates of household violence and abuse can result from traumatic bonding. Traumatic bonding is a survival strategy when the victim sees the abuser as the source of relief from the pain they inflict (Van der Kolk, 1989; Zoppi, 2023). Remember from Chapter 1 that traumatic events are stored in the part of the brain associated with non-verbal memories. How does the brain communicate if not through words? Actions! Victims may grow up to be abusers themselves or may seek similar relationships to the one they had as the victim. And thus, the cycle of abuse is perpetuated into the next generation (Bloom, 1999).

Self-soothing comes from healthy attachments as children. In the absence of a nurturing caregiver at residential school, a survivor may suffer anxiety and attempt to self-soothe by turning to drugs or alcohol in adulthood (Dayton, 2000). It would be foolish to think that such victims could then form healthy attachments to their own children.

The chronic activation of the HPA axis due to the environment at residential schools can result in cortisol depletion. Without cortisol to tamp down adrenaline and noradrenaline in the next stress response, an exaggerated startle response may result (Dayton, 2000; Lehrner & Yehuda, 2018; Mason et al., 1988; Yehuda, 2009). This results in a victim going from '0–100' in a heartbeat. Family members learn to walk on eggshells, producing anxiety-ridden households. Being raised in an environment of abuse, neglect, and household dysfunction may lead to depression, and depression may lead to suicide or suicide ideation (Cronholm et al., 2015; Toombs et al., 2022).

Bougie and Senécal (2010) analyzed data that had been collected from the 2006 Aboriginal Peoples Survey. The negative intergenerational effect of parent-residential schooling on children's school success, particularly boys and older children, was partly attributable to household characteristics and economic status. Former residential school attendees living off reserve were more likely to live in lower-income households and larger households, and suffer food insecurities.

First Nations children of residential school survivors also reported various forms of abuse and neglect, as well as parental mental illness and substance abuse, because altered norms for parenting had developed. These ACEs were partly responsible for their higher levels of depression (Bombay et al., 2011). In addition to increased exposure to ACEs, children of residential school survivors show lower tolerance to stressors. As discussed in Chapter 1, exposure to chronic stress alters HPA axis functioning and changes brain connections as well as morphology. Mothers were more likely to smoke during pregnancy and thus were more likely to deliver babies of lower birth weight (Smylie et al., 2012, p. 432).

First Nations and the Courts

In short, the cumulative effects of ACEs across an individual's life and across generations within a culture, coupled with a continued Eurocentric view of justice, means that First Nations, Inuit, and Metis peoples find themselves overrepresented within the Eurocentric Canadian court system (Department of Justice

Canada, n.d.). As seen throughout world history, colonialism in Canada has led to a myriad of negative consequences for the Indigenous Peoples, including '*cultural alienation, territorial dispossession, and socio-economic marginalization*' (Jackson & Canadian Bar Association, 1988).

Sixties Scoop

The practice of removing Indigenous children from their families continued in the 1960s. Babies born to mothers on reserves were routinely 'scooped' up and placed in mostly white, middle-class families. The practice became known as the 'Sixties Scoop' (Johnston & Canadian Council on Social Development, 1983). The removal of these children was in part, based on a Eurocentric view of cultural norms, including parenting, because social workers were not knowledgeable in the cultures of the families they were splitting up (Hanson and Cherkowski, 2024; Sinclair, 2007). Incidentally, there is an argument to be made about the Eurocentric view of Attachment Theory; the individualistic nature of the Eurocentric caregiver-child relationship may not apply to the collectivist nature of Indigenous families. Second, residential school survivors found themselves living in poverty, and this increased the likelihood of social workers removing their children (Choate et al., 2020). Money for food and care went to foster families.

Further, the practice of simply removing the children delayed the need to address the issues that were making families vulnerable to poverty and dysfunction in the first place (Tait et al., 2013). Incidentally, some countries are currently grappling with an influx of refugee families for the first time. To address their concept of what is in the best interest of the child, some have begun to remove children from their families and place them in families of the majority population (Chak, 2022).

Inuit Housing Today

In late 2022, Marie-Josée Houle, an advocate for federal housing, visited northern Canadian communities in Nunavut and

Newfoundland/Labrador. She observed that more than half of the Inuit, living in their traditional territories, resided in over-crowded accommodations; some were forced to sleep on a rotational schedule, and nearly one-third lived in homes that required major repairs. Some did not have water; some were contaminated with mold due to leaky bathrooms. Overcrowding and unsanitary conditions resulted in a rate of tuberculosis 300 times higher than non-Indigenous Canadians. Heating a home with oil cost $500 per month in the community of Rankin Inlet where 3,000 people live. Sleeping in cars or tents was not unheard of, even in the winter months. Lack of affordable and adequate housing compounded the problems for those with addiction and other mental health issues and also increased the likelihood that children would be removed from the home (Passafiume, 2023).

Slavery and Its Legacy in the USA

We would be remiss if we left this chapter without address-ing the legacy of slavery in the United States. The term 'Post-Traumatic Slave Syndrome' (PTSS) is a theory proposed by Dr. Joyce DeGruy (2018) to describe the effects of trauma experi-enced by African Americans from the slave trade to the recent deaths of unarmed African Americans by white police officers (nugget). The symptoms, while similar to those of PTSD, are spe-cific to the African American experience (DeGruy-Leary, 2018). The 13th Amendment did not end the colonists' use and abuse of the African American people. It was followed by sharecropping, which kept the newly freed slaves working at the landlords' whims. Through deliberate deceit by the landowners, sharecrop-pers found themselves in debt. The federal government turned a blind eye to the issue of Black voter rights, and thus it was impossible for them to change the system (Hinson & Robinson, 2008; Pollard, 2012).

Lynching became another way of keeping Black people sub-servient and fearful of white people. In most cases, the public murder, which was sometimes preceded by torture or muti-lation, was carried out by mobs who concocted charges and rendered a verdict without due process. Often, the allegation was of rape or some other transgression against a white woman. This served to perpetuate the notion that Black men were dangerous predators, and it served to maintain the social separation and respect that fit white people's comfort level. Other charges, such as theft, could result in lynching. Black women were also lynched, as were immigrants or those who were simply opposed to the concept of lynching (National Association for the Advancement of Colored People, 2022).

The government engaged in convict leasing to build railroads and to work in the mines, factories, and lumber camps. They also sent convicts to the plantations that had been emptied of slave labor. This greatly benefited both the government and business owners. 'Crime hunters' were paid for each criminal arrested, and the number of arrests made rose and fell with the need for various forms of labor (Terrell, 2021). Even if found not guilty, a man could be sent to prison if he couldn't pay the legal bills. The convicts were mostly Black men who found themselves in prison because of vagrancy laws that colonists had brought from Europe. The laws were a branch of the Black Codes, which governed many aspects of free Black people's lives (Browne, 2007; History.com Editors, 2023). Prison populations in the South grew dramatically as the lucrative practice gained popularity. Much of the country's infrastructure was built on this exploitative system (Terrell, 2021).

The convict leasing system, with all its abuses, eventually evolved into another cheap labor system: chain gangs. Chain gangs were groups of prisoners chained together and sent out to work on farms or roadways. Because they were chained together, they required less supervision from guards. The chains were heavy and often created ulcers around the ankles. The prisoners worked at gunpoint and were whipped into submission. These later forms of government abuses ended in the 1950s (Browne, 2007; Chain Gangs, 2024).

From the 1930s to the 1960s, the federal government encouraged segregation in the form of redlining certain neighborhoods, which led to an increase in urban decay (Egede et al., 2023). Minorities were unable to access credit despite being qualified. As the years passed, the differences in equity appreciation became greater. The urban minority-filled neighborhoods became poorer, and the inhabitants and their children received different levels of education since school funding was sometimes based on property values (Guastaferro, 2020). In an article for the School of Public Health at Berkley, Nadia Lathan investigated how areas that were once redlined today show increased pollution. The inhabitants suffer from more health issues and are served by fewer amenities (Lathan, 2023).

The Black Lives Matter protests began in May 2020 after the death of George Floyd during a police encounter. Weeks after Mr. Floyd's death, the results of a 4-year study on police encounter death rates of Black vs. White Americans were published in PLOS ONE. While the rates differed based on location, the study did find that, on average, Black people were over three times as likely to be killed during a police encounter as white people (Haynes, 2020). And the legacy continues.

Break Time #2! Regardless of the context, how many ACEs could you count for a hypothetical (or actual) descendant of a trauma survivor?

ACE	✔
Physical Abuse	
Sexual Abuse	
Emotional Abuse	
Physical Neglect	
Emotional Neglect	
Divorce	
Substance Abuse	
Interpersonal Violence	
Incarcerated Relative	
Mental Illness	
Living in Foster Care	
Community Violence	
Racism	
Neighborhood Safety (lack of)	
Bullying	

Behavior is learned through social interactions and reinforcement. Some survivors of colonialism experienced trauma that they then passed on to the next generation. Whether prenatal or postnatal, parents convey messages to their children about the world they will be/are living in. As outlined in this chapter, the messages come to your students in many ways. Knowing your students' personal histories, and even those of their parents, can provide valuable insights into how best to meet their academic, social, and emotional needs (nugget). Pay close attention to Dr. Stembridge's project in the section on Culturally Responsive Teaching in Chapter 3!

Answers to Brain Breaks

Break Time #2! Regardless of the context, how many ACEs could you count for a hypothetical (or actual) descendant of a trauma survivor?

ACE	✔
Physical Abuse	✔
Sexual Abuse	✔
Emotional Abuse	✔
Physical Neglect	✔
Emotional Neglect	✔
Divorce	
Substance Abuse	✔
Interpersonal Violence	✔
Incarcerated Relative	✔
Mental Illness	✔
Living in Foster Care	✔
Community Violence	✔
Racism	✔
Neighborhood Safety (lack of)	✔
Bullying	

Note: We did not specifically discuss divorce or bullying. Could they be implied?

Notes

1 https://www.cdc.gov/ncbddd/fasd/facts.html.
2 https://www.hhs.gov/sites/default/files/consequences-smoking-consumer-guide.pdf.

References

Ackerman, C. (2023, April 19). *What is attachment theory? Bowlby's 4 stages explained*. PositivePsychology.com. https://positivepsychology.com/attachment-theory/

Agular, W., & Halseth, R. (2015). *Aboriginal peoples and historic trauma: The process of intergenerational transmission*. National Collaborating Centre for Aboriginal Health. https://www.ccnsa-nccah.ca/docs/context/RPT-HistoricTrauma-IntergenTransmission-Aguiar-Halseth-EN.pdf

American Psychological Association. (2023, November 15). *APA dictionary of psychology*. American Psychological Association. https://dictionary.apa.org/intergenerational-trauma

Bandura, A. (1977). *Social learning theory*. Prentice Hall.

Bloom, S. (1999). *Trauma theory abbreviated – pbworks*. Trauma Theory Abbreviated. http://iheartenglish.pbworks.com/f/Trauma+Theory+Explained+14+pages.pdf

Bombay, A., Matheson, K., & Anisman, H. (2011). The impact of stressors on second generation Indian residential school survivors. *Transcultural Psychiatry*. https://doi.org/10.1177/1363461511410240

Bombay, A., Matheson, K., & Anisman, H. (2014). The intergenerational effects of Indian Residential Schools: Implications for the concept of historical trauma. *Transcultural Psychiatry*, *51*(3), 320–338. https://doi.org/10.1177/1363461513503380

Bougie, Evelyne and Senécal, Sacha (2010) Registered Indian children's school success and intergenerational effects of residential schooling in Canada. *The International Indigenous Policy Journal*, *1*(1), Article 5. Available at: http://ir.lib.uwo.ca/iipj/vol1/iss1/5

Brave Heart, M. Y. (2003). The historical trauma response among natives and its relationship with substance abuse: A Lakota illustration.

Journal of Psychoactive drugs, *35*(1), 7–13. https://doi.org/10.1080/ 02791072.2003.10399988

Bretherton, I. (1992). The origins of attachment theory: John Bowlby and Mary Ainsworth. *Developmental Psychology*, *28*(5), 759–775. https:// doi.org/10.1037/0012-1649.28.5.759

Browne, J. (2007). *Rooted in slavery: Prison labor exploitation*. Rooted in Slavery: Prison Labor Exploitation | Reimagine! https://www. reimaginerpe.org/node/856

Centers for Disease Control and Prevention. (2022, November 1). *Health problems caused by secondhand smoke*. Centers for Disease Control and Prevention. https://www.cdc.gov/tobacco/secondhand-smoke/ health.html#:~:text=Children%20who%20are%20exposed%20 to,symptoms%2C%20and%20slowed%20lung%20growt

Centers for Disease Control and Prevention Office on Smoking and Health. (2014, January). *Department of Health & Human Services | HHS.gov*. https://www.hhs.gov/sites/default/files/consequences- smoking-consumer-guide.pdf

Chain Gangs. *Encyclopedia of race and racism*. Retrieved January 08, 2024 from Encyclopedia.com: https://www.encyclopedia.com/ social-sciences/encyclopedias-almanacs-transcripts-and-maps/ chain-gangs

Chak, F. M. (2022, February 23). Stealing innocence: The theft of refu- gee children in Sweden. *Politics Today*. https://politicstoday.org/ stealing-innocence-the-theft-of-refugee-children-in-sweden/

Cherry, K. (2023, February 22). How attachment theory works. *Verywell Mind*. https://www.verywellmind.com/what-is-attachment-theory- 2795337

Choate, P. W., CrazyBull, B., Lindstrom, D., & Lindstrom, G. (2020). Where do we go from here?: Ongoing colonialism from attachment the- ory. *Aotearoa New Zealand Social Work*, *32*(1), 32–44. https://search. informit.org/doi/10.3316/informit.080103162065454

Coates, K. (2008, May). *NCFNG | The Indian act and the future of Aboriginal Governance in Canada*. https://fngovernance.org/wp-content/ uploads/2020/05/coates.pdf

Cortés-Albornoz, M. C., García-Guáqueta, D. P., & Talero-Gutiérrez, C. (2021). Maternal nutrition and neurodevelopment: A scoping review. *Nutrients*, *13*(10). https://doi.org/10.3390/nu13103530

Coussons-Read, M. E. (2013). Effects of prenatal stress on pregnancy and human development: Mechanisms and pathways. *Obstetric Medicine, 6*(2), 52–57. https://doi.org/10.1177/1753495X12473751

Cronholm, P. F., Forke, C. M., Wade, R., Bair-Merritt, M. H., Davis, M., Harkins-Schwarz, M., Pachter, L. M., & Fein, J. A. (2015). Adverse childhood experiences: Expanding the concept of adversity. *American Journal of Preventive Medicine, 49*(3), 354–361. https://doi.org/10.1016/j.amepre.2015.02.001

Davin, N. F. (1879). (rep.). *Report on industrial schools for Indians and half-breeds* (pp. 1–17). Ottawa, Ontario. Retrieved January 16, 2024, from https://dev.nctr.ca/wp-content/uploads/2021/01/Davin-Report.pdf

Dayton, T. (2000). *Trauma and addiction: Ending the cycle of pain through emotional literacy.* Health Communications Inc.

De Rooij, S. R., Bleker, L. S., Painter, R. C., Ravelli, A. C., & Roseboom, T. J. (2021, May 5). *Lessons learned from 25 years of research into long term consequences of prenatal exposure to the Dutch famine 1944–45: The Dutch famine birth cohort.* International Journal of Environmental Health Research. https://pubmed.ncbi.nlm.nih.gov/33949901/

deBruin, T. (2020, April 29). Canada and the Dutch Hunger winter. *The Canadian Encyclopedia.* https://www.thecanadianencyclopedia.ca/en/article/canada-and-the-dutch-hunger-winter

DeGruy-Leary, J. (2018). *Post traumatic slave syndrome: America's legacy of enduring injury and healing.* Joy DeGruy Publications Inc.

Department of Justice Canada. (n.d.). *Federal Accountability Act.* Retrieved June 2, 2024, from https://laws.justice.gc.ca/eng/acts/F-11.73/index.html

Di, H. K., Gan, Y., Lu, K., Wang, C., Zhu, Y., Meng, X., Xia, W. Q., Xu, M. Z., Feng, J., Tian, Q. F., He, Y., Nie, Z. Q., Liu, J. A., Song, F. J., & Lu, Z. X. (2022). Maternal smoking status during pregnancy and low birth weight in offspring: Systematic review and meta-analysis of 55 cohort studies published from 1986 to 2020. *World Journal of Pediatrics: WJP, 18*(3), 176–185. https://doi.org/10.1007/s12519-021-00501-5

Dwyer, J. B., McQuown, S. C., & Leslie, F. M. (2009). The dynamic effects of nicotine on the developing brain. *Pharmacology & Therapeutics, 122*(2), 125–139. https://doi.org/10.1016/j.pharmthera.2009.02.003

Dziurkowska, E., & Wesolowski, M. (2021). Cortisol as a biomarker of mental disorder severity. *Journal of Clinical Medicine*, *10*(21). https://doi.org/10.3390/jcm10215204

Egede, L. E., Walker, R. J., Campbell, J. A., Linde, S., Hawks, L. C., & Burgess, K. M. (2023). Modern day consequences of historic redlining: Finding a path forward. *Journal of General Internal Medicine*, *38*(6), 1534–1537. https://doi.org/10.1007/s11606-023-08051-4

Ernst, M., Moolchan, E. T., & Robinson, M. L. (2001). Behavioral and neural consequences of prenatal exposure to nicotine. *Journal of the American Academy of Child and Adolescent Psychiatry*, *40*(6), 630–641. https://doi.org/10.1097/00004583-200106000-00007

Evans, S. E., Davies, C., & DiLillo, D. (2008). Exposure to domestic violence: A meta-analysis of child and adolescent outcomes. *Aggression and Violent Behavior*, *13*(2), 131–140. https://doi.org/10.1016/j.avb.2008.02.005

Faulk, Christopher, & Dolinoy, Dana C. (2011). *Timing is everything*. *Epigenetics*, *6*(7), 791–797. https://doi.org/10.4161/epi.6.7.16209

Ferguson, M. (2023, September 30). The intergenerational cost of the residential school system. *Penticton Herald*. https://www.pentictonherald.ca/spare_news/article_2290ae21-7496-5b97-9d4a-db33aa92aa1a.html

Fraley, R. C. (2010). *A brief overview of adult attachment theory and research*. University of Illinois. https://internal.psychology.illinois.edu/~rcfraley/attachment.htm

Gershoff, E. T. (2002). Corporal punishment by parents and associated child behaviors and experiences: A meta-analytic and theoretical review. *Psychological Bulletin*, *128*(4), 539–579. https://doi.org/10.1037/0033-2909.128.4.539

Guastaferro, L. (2020, November 2). Why racial inequities in America's schools are rooted in housing policies of the past. *USA Today*.

Günther, V., Alkatout, I., Vollmer, C., Maass, N., Strauss, A., & Voigt, M. (2021). Impact of nicotine and maternal BMI on fetal birth weight. *BMC Pregnancy and Childbirth*, *21*. https://doi.org/10.1186/s12884-021-03593-z

Hanson, K., & Cherkowski, S. (2024). Living in Circle. *Compassionate Leadership for School Improvement and Renewal*, 49.

Hanson, E., Gamez, D. P., & Manuel, A. (2020, September). The residential school system. *indigenousfoundations*. https://indigenous foundations.arts.ubc.ca/the_residential_school_system/

Haynes, D. (2020, June 24). Study: Black Americans 3 times more likely to be killed by police. *UPI*. https://www.upi.com/Top_News/US/2020/06/24/Study-Black-Americans-3-times-more-likely-to-be-killed-by-police/6121592949925/

Heijmans, B. T., Tobi, E. W., Stein, A. D., Putter, H., Blauw, G. J., Susser, E. S., Slagboom, P. E., & Lumey, L. H. (2008). Persistent epigenetic differences associated with prenatal exposure to famine in humans. *Proceedings of the National Academy of Sciences of the United States of America*, *105*(44), 17046–17049. https://doi.org/10.1073/pnas.0806560105

Hellemans, K. G., Sliwowska, J. H., Verma, P., & Weinberg, J. (2010). Prenatal alcohol exposure: Fetal programming and later life vulnerability to stress, depression and anxiety disorders. *Neuroscience & Biobehavioral Reviews*, *34*(6), 791–807. https://doi.org/10.1016/j.neubiorev.2009.06.004

Hinson, W. & Robinson, E. (2008). "We didn't get nothing:" The plight of black farmers. *Journal of African American Studies*, 12. 283–302.

History.com Editors. (2023, March 29). *Black codes – Definition, dates & Jim Crow laws*. https://www.history.com/topics/black-history/black-codes

Horwood, J., Mogridge, N., & Darlow, B. (1999). Cognitive, educational, and behavioural outcomes at 7 to 8 years. *Archives of Disease in Childhood. Fetal and Neonatal Edition*, *80*(1), F78. https://doi.org/10.1136/fn.80.1.f78a

Jackson, M., & Canadian Bar Association. (1988). Locking up natives in Canada: A report of the committee of the Canadian bar association on imprisonment and release: Worldcat.org. *OCLC WorldCat.org*. https://search.worldcat.org/title/Locking-up-natives-in-Canada-:-a-report-of-the-Committee-of-the-Canadian-Bar-Association-on-Imprisonment-and-Release/oclc/31661340

Johnston, P., & Canadian Council on Social Development. (1983). *Native children and the child welfare system*. Canadian Council on Social

Development in association with James Lorimer. Retrieved January 16 2024 from https://www.deslibris.ca/ID/413616

Josewski, V., de Leeuw, S., & Greenwood, M. (2023). Grounding wellness: Coloniality, placeism, land, and a critique of "social" determinants of indigenous mental health in the Canadian context. *International Journal of Environmental Research and Public Health, 20*(5), 4319. https://doi.org/10.3390/ijerph20054319

Kennedy, J. H., & Kennedy, C. E. (2004). Attachment theory: Implications for school psychology. *Psychology in the Schools, 41*(2), 247–259. https://doi.org/10.1002/pits.10153

Kwon, E. J., & Kim, Y. J. (2017, November). What is fetal programming?: A lifetime health is under the control of in utero health. *Obstetrics & Gynecology Science.* https://www.ncbi.nlm.nih.gov/pmc/articles/PMC5694724/

Lathan, N. (2023, September 20). *50 years after being outlawed, redlining still drives neighborhood health inequities.* UC Berkeley Public Health. https://publichealth.berkeley.edu/news-media/research-highlights/50-years-after-being-outlawed-redlining-still-drives-neighborhood-health-inequities/#:~:text=Although%20the%20practice%20has%20been,more%20than%2050%20years%20later

Lehrner, A., & Yehuda, R. (2018). Cultural trauma and epigenetic inheritance. *Development and Psychopathology, 30*(5), 1763–1777. https://doi.org/10.1017/S0954579418001153

Maple-Brown, L. J., & Hampton, D. (2020, May). *Indigenous cultures in countries with similar colonisation histories.* https://www.thelancet.com/journals/langlo/article/PIIS2214-109X(20)30072-3/fulltext

Mason, J. W., Giller, E. L., Kosten, T. R., & Harkness, L. (1988, August). Elevation of urinary norepinephrine/cortisol ratio in posttraumatic stress disorder. *The Journal of Nervous and Mental Disease, 176*(8), 498–502.

McLeod, S. (2023, October 24). *Albert Bandura's social learning theory in psychology.* Simply Psychology. https://www.simplypsychology.org/bandura.html

Menzies, P. (2024). Intergenerational trauma and residential schools. In *The Canadian Encyclopedia.* Retrieved from https://www.thecanadianencyclopedia.ca/en/article/intergenerational-trauma-and-residential-schools

Miller, J. (2024). Residential schools in Canada. In *The Canadian Encyclopedia*. Retrieved from https://www.thecanadianencyclopedia.ca/en/article/residential-schools

Milloy, J. (2008, May). *NCNFG | Indian act colonialism: A century of dishonour, 1869–1969*. https://fngovernance.org/wp-content/uploads/2020/09/milloy.pdf

Milot, T., Éthier, L. S., St-Laurent, D., & Provost, M. A. (2010). The role of trauma symptoms in the development of behavioral problems in maltreated preschoolers. *Child Abuse & Neglect, 34*(4), 225–234. https://doi.org/10.1016/j.chiabu.2009.07.006

NAACP. (2022, February 11). *History of lynching in America*. https://naacp.org/find-resources/history-explained/history-lynching-america

NCTR. (2021, October 26). *Residential school history*. https://nctr.ca/education/teaching-resources/residential-school-history/#:~:text=Children%20were%20harshly%20punished%20for,how%20they%20treated%20the%20children.&text=We%20know%20that%20thousands%20of,be%20home%20with%20their%20families

NCTR. (2023, August 10). *Residential school timeline*. https://nctr.ca/exhibits/residential-school-timeline/

O'Donnell, K. J., Bugge Jensen, A., Freeman, L., Khalife, N., O'Connor, T. G., & Glover, V. (2012). Maternal prenatal anxiety and downregulation of placental 11β-HSD2. *Psychoneuroendocrinology, 37*(6), 818–826. https://doi.org/10.1016/j.psyneuen.2011.09.014

Painter, R. C., Osmond, C., Gluckman, P., Hanson, M., Phillips, D. I., & Roseboom, T. J. (2008). Transgenerational effects of prenatal exposure to the Dutch famine on neonatal adiposity and health in later life. *BJOG: An International Journal of Obstetrics and Gynaecology, 115*(10), 1243–1249. https://doi.org/10.1111/j.1471-0528.2008.01822.x

Passafiume, A. (2023, November 27). *Federal advocate calls Inuit housing conditions a "staggering failure" of government | CBC News*. CBCnews. https://www.cbc.ca/news/canada/north/inuit-housing-crisis-houle-report-1.7041217

Pollard, S. (Director). (2012). *Slavery by another name* [Film]. TPT National Productions.

Popova, S. (2018, April). World Health Organization International Study on the … – CANFASD. *Study on the Prevalence of Fetal Alcohol Spectrum Disorder (FASD)*. https://canfasd.ca/wp-content/uploads/2018/05/2018-Popova-WHO-FASD-Prevalance-Report.pdf

Popova, S., Lange, S., Burd, L., & Rehm, J. (2015, October 21). The economic burden of fetal alcohol spectrum disorder in Canada in 2013. *Alcohol and alcoholism (Oxford, Oxfordshire)*. https://pubmed.ncbi.nlm.nih.gov/26493100/

Public Broadcasting Service. (n.d.). Lynching in America. *PBS*. https://www.pbs.org/wgbh/americanexperience/features/emmett-lynching-america/

Rogers, J. M. (2009). Tobacco and pregnancy. *Reproductive Toxicology*, *28*(2), 152–160. https://doi.org/10.1016/j.reprotox.2009.03.012

Royal Commission on Aboriginal Peoples (RCAP) (1996). *Looking forward, looking back: Report of the royal commission on aboriginal peoples*, Volume 1, Communication Group.

Seim, A. R., Jozefiak, T., Wichstrøm, L. et al. (2022). Reactive attachment disorder and disinhibited social engagement disorder in adolescence: Co-occurring psychopathology and psychosocial problems. *European Child & Adolescent Psychiatry*, *31*, 85–98. https://doi.org/10.1007/s00787-020-01673-7

Sinclair, R. 2007. Identity lost and found: Lessons from the sixties scoop. *First Peoples Child & Family Review*, *3*(1), 65–82. Retrieved from https://fpcfr.com/index.php/FPCFR/article/view/25

Smallwood, R., Woods, C., Power, T., & Usher, K. (2020). Understanding the impact of historical trauma due to colonization on the health and well-being of indigenous young peoples: A systematic scoping review. *Journal of Transcultural Nursing*. https://doi.org/10.1177/1043659620935955

Smylie, J., O'Campo, P., McShane, K., Daoud, N., Davey, C. (2012) Prenatal health. In The First Nations Information Governance Centre (ed) *First nations regional health survey (RHS) phase 2 (2008/10): National report on the adult, youth, and children living in First Nations communities* (pp. 424–439). The First Nations Information Governance Centre.

Stephens, M. A. C., & Wand, G. (2012). Stress and the HPA axis: Role of glucocorticoids in alcohol dependence. *Alcohol Research: Current Reviews.* https://www.ncbi.nlm.nih.gov/pmc/articles/PMC3860380/

Tait, C. L., Henry, R., & Walker, R. L. (2013). *Child welfare: A social determinant of health for Canadian first.* https://journalindigenouswellbeing.co.nz/wp-content/uploads/2013/07/04Tait.pdf

Terrell, E. (2021, June 17). The convict leasing system: Slavery in its worst aspects. *Inside Adams.* January 16, 2024. https://blogs.loc.gov/inside_adams/2021/06/convict-leasing-system/

Thau, L., Gandhi, J., & Sharma, S. (2023, August 28). Physiology, cortisol – Statpearls – NCBI bookshelf. *Physiology, Cortisol.* https://www.ncbi.nlm.nih.gov/books/NBK538239/

Toombs, E., Lund, J. I., Mushquash, A. R., & Mushquash, C. J. (2022). Intergenerational residential school attendance and increased substance use among First Nation adults living off-reserve: An analysis of the aboriginal peoples survey 2017. *Frontiers in Public Health, 10.* https://doi.org/10.3389/fpubh.2022.1029139

Union of Ontario Indians. (2013). *An overview of the Indian residential school system – Anishinabek.* https://www.anishinabek.ca/wp-content/uploads/2016/07/An-Overview-of-the-IRS-System-Booklet.pdf

van der Kolk, B. A. (1989). The compulsion to repeat the trauma. Re-enactment, revictimization, and masochism. *The Psychiatric Clinics of North America, 12*(2), 389–411.

Yehuda, R. (2009). Status of glucocorticoid alterations in post-traumatic stress disorder. *Annals of the New York Academy of Sciences, 1179,* 56–69. https://doi.org/10.1111/j.1749-6632.2009.04979.x

Yehuda, R. (2022, July 1). How parents' trauma leaves biological traces in children. *Scientific American.* https://www.scientificamerican.com/article/how-parents-rsquo-trauma-leaves-biological-traces-in-children/

Yehuda, R., & Lehrner, A. (2018, October). Intergenerational transmission of trauma effects: Putative role of epigenetic mechanisms. *World Psychiatry: Official Journal of the World Psychiatric Association*

(WPA). https://www.ncbi.nlm.nih.gov/pmc/articles/PMC6127768/#:~: text=Epigenetic%20mechanisms%20have%20been%20favored, paternal%20trauma%20exposure

Zoppi, L. (2023, April 25). Trauma bonding: Definition, examples, signs, and recovery. *Medical News Today*. https://www.medicalnewstoday. com/articles/trauma-bonding#:~:text=Trauma%20bonding%20 occurs%20when%20a,the%20abuser's%20behavior%20will%20 change

Part 2
The How

3

Culture

The movement of people from their homelands, whether voluntarily or forced, has meant that our classrooms are becoming ever more diverse. In fact, millions of children have emigrated since the start of the 21st century (McBrien, 2022). These students exist on a continuum. At one end are the students who are already fluent in your language and who have received a compatible education without any disruptions. At the other end are children who cannot speak a word of your language and have never had the opportunity to go to school. So, their gaps in achievement may be small or large, just don't confuse them with gaps in ability.

Members of all ethnic minorities, including those who have faced disruptions due to historical trauma, face special challenges within the education system, which has been normed to the dominant Eurocentric culture (Bushnell, 2021; Ciuffetelli Parker & Conversano, 2021). Special challenges may include systemic biases in content and testing as well as a lack of cultural competence or cultural humility on the part of the teacher. This may lead to inaccurate assessments of these students' abilities and reasons for behaviors (Pit-ten Cate & Glock, 2018; Kreskow, 2013; Singh, 1970).

To close gaps, we must do all we can to create an equitable learning environment for all students. Let's take a moment to consider an important word in that last sentence: *equitable*. Equitable and equal are not the same. In an equal learning environment, all students are treated as equals, although they are clearly not; they are all given the exact same resources to learn with and

DOI: 10.4324/9781032707945-6

from. In an equitable learning environment, students receive resources that take into account their personal strengths, needs, and histories.

Some well-meaning educators believe that color-blindness and/or culture-blindness will lessen issues facing minorities in their classrooms. This is a misconception that may inadvertently further disadvantage those very same students. Acknowledging and leveraging those differences will engage their attention and increase their commitment to their own learning (Kaiser & Rasminsky, 2020). Again, equal is not equitable (nugget).

Biases

Unconscious Bias

So, what happens when we see someone of a different culture? The primitive part of our brain, or reptilian brain, does what it has always done to keep us safe and it does it without conscious thought. It monitors the incoming stimulus, which is now the face of a person, and rates the threat level. If the person is like us (same race, same age, same gender, etc.), the brain sees them as being safer than if they are not like us. Our brain recalls similar experiences and then decides, based on those past experiences, how to proceed with this new stimulus. But what if those previous experiences were based on biases or stereotyping?

Before reading further, watch the video called *The Neuroscience of Unconscious Bias* (Bhasin Consulting)[1] or follow these steps:

1. Go to YouTube.
2. Look for '*The Neuroscience of Unconscious Bias*' by Bhasin Consulting Inc.

After all, we are no longer talking about a predator; we are talking about a person, perhaps a student, parent, or colleague. It is important to take a moment and engage the thinking part of our brain to become aware of our unconscious/implicit bias. Being aware of it means we are less likely to repeat it.

If you are still unsure, you can also watch the video called *How to Check Your Unconscious Bias*.[2] Hard-copy readers, follow these steps to access the video:

1. Go to YouTube.
2. Look up: *'How to Check Your Unconscious Bias'* by Jennifer Eberhardt.

Do you think you have bias? If you have a brain, you do! Here is a bias test written by Harvard University. It may have an American or Canadian flavor to it depending on which you select. It is not perfect but it may give you an indication of your own unconscious biases. Each takes about 10 minutes. The test is called the Harvard Implicit Association Test[3] or the Canadian version in either official language, Implicit Association Test (Canada).[4] Hard-copy readers, here are your steps:

1. Google Harvard IAT or Harvard IAT Canada.
2. At the bottom of the home page, select 'I wish to proceed.'
3. Select a relevant test.

Resource Bias

Now that you have assessed your own biases, consider the resources in your classrooms. Do they show biases? You can use a checklist like this one from Nova Scotia's Department of Education and Early Childhood Development (EECD). The actual checklist is on pages 4–6. You can print them out. The checklist is called the Bias Evaluation Instrument.[5]

Follow these steps to access it:

1. Google Bias Evaluation Instrument Nova Scotia.
2. Read the rationale on page 2.
3. Use the checklist on the last three pages.

Deficit Thinking

In an attempt to explain why the learning gaps are not closing, you may turn to *deficit thinking*, which is a result of implicit bias (Patton Davis & Museus, 2019). Deficit thinking is really excuse-making. Creating a narrative in which minority students or students of low income are inherently limited and shifts the blame for academic failure from the educational system to the student, their family, their culture, and their socioeconomic level (Valencia, 2010). When a student gets the message that they are inherently limited, they may develop a fixed mindset of 'I can't.' If our fate was decided for us at a young age by factors over which we have no control, how interested in engaging in learning would we be?

What can we do? For starters, we can shift our focus from our students' deficits to their assets. Nurturing their strengths as well as their potential will enable them to develop a growth mindset and empower them to reach their full academic and personal potential. Our culturally diverse learners bring knowledge and experiences that can enrich the learning environment for everyone, including you. Feelings of acceptance and belonging will help students get ready for learning (nugget).

Break Time #3A! Let's see how well you can shift from deficit thinking to asset thinking.

Na-Moo is a 10-year-old South Korean student who chose Ivy as her Canadian name. I was told that Ivy had some understanding of English. Her peers and I welcomed her with smiles and attempted to communicate with her. As time has passed, I have noticed that she rarely makes eye contact with me; eye contact with her classmates is also rare. When she does speak, it is usually after a period of silence, which can be awkward. Even then, her face rarely changes expression. Yet, Na-Moo smiles and even laughs at odd times.

Deficit Thinking	*Asset Thinking*
Na-Moo is uncomfortable.	
Na-Moo's command of our language is not as good as I thought.	
Na-Moo seems unemotional or disengaged when speaking.	
Na-Moo needs to be assessed by our School Team or Guidance Counselor.	

For help filling in the right side, do a bit of reading at the website called South Korean Culture-Communication.[6] To access it, follow these steps:

1. Google 'Cultural Atlas.'
2. In the search bar, type South Korean communication (by Nina Evason).

Be sure to check your answers at the back of the chapter!

Ethnocentrism

What else can you do? You can be aware of ethnocentrism vs. cultural relativism. Judging another culture as being wrong or inferior while viewing our own culture as being correct and/or superior is *ethnocentrism*. Conversely, viewing all cultures as being valid and/or equal to our own is *cultural relativism* (nugget). There is a video called *Ethnocentrism Examples Animated Review*.[7] Follow these steps to watch it:

1. Go to YouTube.
2. Search 'FunSimpleLIFE Ethnocentrism.'

Break Time #3B: Ethnocentrism vs. Cultural Relativism
Maryem is a grade 6 student who arrived in Canada in early January after leaving Syria with her family. Initially, her Canadian teacher was pleased to see that Maryem demonstrated good social skills, was engaged in her classwork, and showed interest in the school's extracurricular activities. However, after a few months, Maryem started to look pale and tired. She became withdrawn. Eventually, Maryem started to put her head on her desk. Because a change in Maryem's behavior and productivity occurred, the teacher called her home. The teacher was told that Maryem and her family were three weeks into the holy month of Ramadan.

Ethnocentrism	*Cultural Relativism*
It is wrong/cruel for a child to be fasting all day.	
Because of this fasting, Maryem is now disengaging from everyone for much of her school day. It looks as though she has stopped caring.	

For help, again, do a bit of reading at the site called What to Know About Ramadan and How Refugees Celebrate.[8] Google 'UNHCR What to Know About Ramadan and How Refugees Celebrate.'

Trust

Let's recap. We know that our classrooms are becoming more culturally diverse. We know that we have implicit biases that can, if left unchecked, negatively impact how we interact with our students and taint their learning environment. As teachers, it is up to us to shift our paradigms; it is not up to our students to fit into the existing model. We can start by considering our little newcomers from an asset-based perspective and view their cultures through their eyes. That's a good start, but then what can we do?

The relationships between and among all stakeholders, including teachers, students, parents, colleagues, and administration, must be predicated on trust. Trust is key. In his book, *The Speed of Trust*, Stephen Covey defines trust as being 'the feeling of confidence that we have in another's character and competence' (Covey & Merrill, 2018). In terms of character, are we people of our word? Are our intentions good? In terms of competence, do we actually know what we are doing? Do our students believe that we can really help them reach their fullest potential?

In his book *Teaching Life: Our Calling, Our Choices, Our Challenges* (2019), Armand Doucet describes a great school culture as one of 'valuing human resources, treating everybody with trust, instilling a sense of competence and cohesion to solve any obstacle.' His 'go slow to go fast' approach requires investing time at the beginning of the year in the very deliberate development of trusting relationships between him and his students. Only then are they ready to push learning boundaries and take risks. While doing so, he creates an environment where his students learn how to learn.

When our students truly believe they can trust us, their brains release three important chemicals: dopamine, serotonin, and oxytocin. Working together, these chemicals allow for better,

higher-level learning because they can downgrade the functioning of the amygdala while upgrading the functioning of the prefrontal cortex (Glaser, 2014). Consider the image in Figure 3.1
from Dr. Loretta Breuning of *The Inner Mammal Institute*. A bond
is produced between the listener and the speaker thanks to

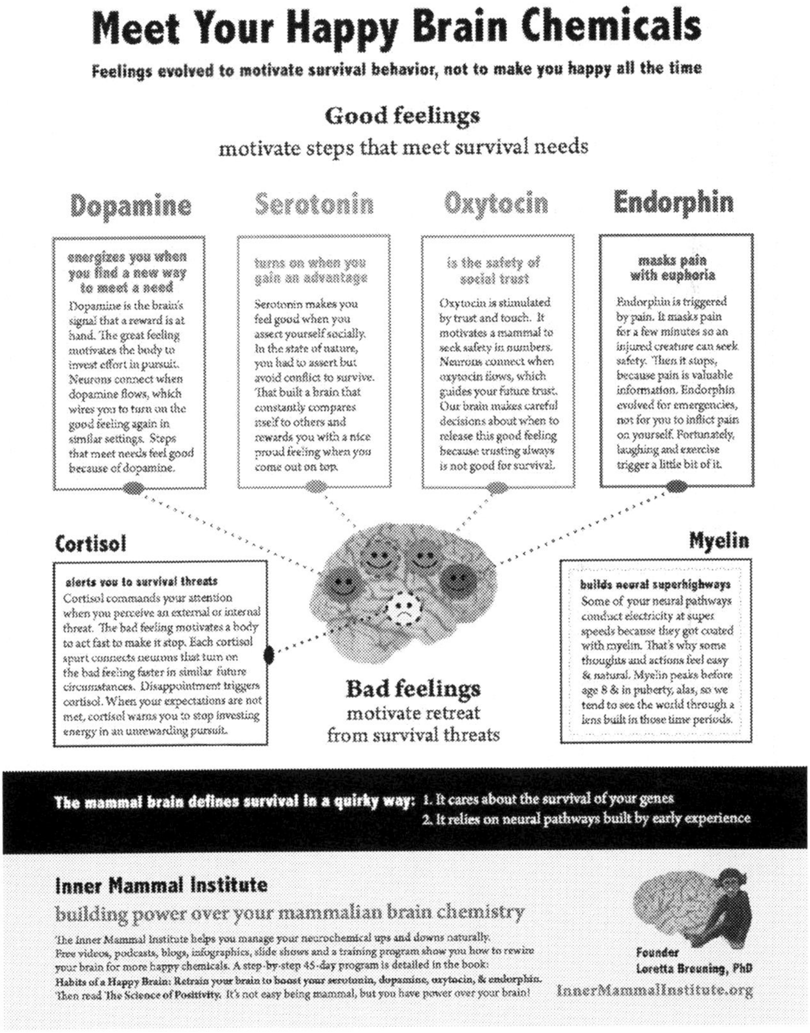

FIGURE 3.1 Happy Brain Chemicals

Source: Loretta Breuning, *Inner Mammal Institute*, https://innermammalinstitute.org/

oxytocin, while dopamine and serotonin contribute to motivation and pride. This is exactly what we want for our students
(nugget). Note the negative impact of distrust. Remember from
Chapter 1 that cortisol impairs the functioning of the prefrontal
cortex. Incidentally, the prefrontal cortex contains mirror neurons that generate the important emotion known as empathy, but
more on that later!

Cultural Humility and Cultural Competence

So far in this chapter, we have asked, *What (else) can we do*? three
times. Well, we are asking a fourth time: what else can we do?

Understanding, on a conceptual level, specific cultures and
altering your teaching methods accordingly is *cultural competence*.
It implies acquiring a discrete body of knowledge, which in turn
implies a finite amount of time. A way to cultural competence
is via cultural humility, which is not so much a skill set as it is a
mindset. Dr. Melanie Tervalon and Dr. Jann Murray-García (1998)
originally coined the term *cultural humility* for the medical profession about a lifelong process of self-awareness and learning to
rectify biases in the physician-patient relationship (Tervalon &
Murray-García, 1998).

To put it another way, cultural humility is an examination of
our own beliefs, values, and norms while recognizing we cannot
completely understand the perspectives of our students, parents,
and colleagues who have grown up in a culture different from our
own. As we explore and learn about our students' cultures, we
can reach cultural competence, enabling us to work effectively
with them while recognizing we will never fully understand the
perspective of another's cultural beliefs. Recognizing how the
dominant culture views the minority cultures is key to creating a
new and unbiased view of the minority cultures (nugget).

Break Time #3C! Your Cultural Humility

Please pause and carefully reflect upon how you interact with
others, including your students, before rating yourself. The questionnaire is printable and worth printing. There is a place at the
end to consider your strengths and areas you would like to work

on. Acknowledge that everyone has biases, that's okay, and that developing true cultural humility is a lifelong process. There is a Cultural Humility Self-Reflection Tool for School Staff.[9] Google 'School Mental Health Ontario Cultural Humility Self-Reflection for School Staff' (with permission from Central Toronto Youth Services (CTYS) Cultural Humility Self-Assessment Self-Reflection Tool, originally from Greater Vancouver Island Multicultural Society, Western University, and the Government of Canada Cultural Competence Self-Assessment Self-Reflection Tool).

We hope that you actually did that self-reflection. Understanding how culture affects students' learning and behaviors, especially if it contains histories of oppression and genocide, is necessary if we are to assist them in reaching their full potential. But to do that, we must first understand our own culture, particularly if it is the dominant Eurocentric culture of the educational system. Understanding how one's culture has historically viewed the different cultures in the classroom is key to redressing it.

Case Study: Forest Glen School (K–4) Moncton, New Brunswick, Canada

Between 2016 and 2021, the population of Moncton, New Brunswick, experienced a growth rate of 10.5%, representing an additional 7,581 people, resulting in an overall population of 74,470. Most significantly for us, the growth rate in the 0- to 14-year-old population was one of the fastest in the nation at 11.3% (Jupia Consultants Inc., 2023).

This large influx of culturally diverse learners to New Brunswick schools necessitated the creation of EAL (English as an Additional Language) support positions. One such school is Forest Glen School, which has a population of about 375 students between kindergarten and grade 4. Before 2016, the student population primarily consisted of white, English-speaking children. Today, the school has students from 36 different countries who speak 25 different languages. Currently, over 50% of the students were not born in Canada. These MLL (Multilingual

Learners) receive support from their EST (Educational Support Team) member, Mrs. Candace Douglass.

Candace had been a grade 1 teacher at the same school before being asked to take on this new role. She recognized that the predominantly white, Canadian-born staff did not represent the student population and, like all of us, had biases. She wanted to make sure that the school was doing everything it could to promote awareness and inclusion so that the students felt safe, valued, and respected. Toward that end, Candace created *Culture Club*, a weekly lunchtime opportunity for students to learn from and about each other. Candace believes that the school's diversity is its strength and that each student's unique background can be leveraged to create an accepting, respectful, and open learning environment for everyone. She feels that in learning about one another, students can develop deeper relationships and greater empathy. The reciprocal nature of the interactions means that the club also includes Canadian-born students.

The program is new to Candace as well as the club members, so she is learning right along with her students. She began with a culture *Show and Tell* and role-modeled for the students by telling them about herself, her beliefs, the food she eats, and the traditions of her culture. She brought in pictures for the students to look at. Not only is the club a voluntary activity but so is participation. Students who wish to present their culture can do so individually or in groups. To the best of her ability, she schedules presentations to be in sync with the multicultural calendar. For example, during Diwali, students from India share their culture. This adds another level of authenticity for her young students.

I was invited by Candace to visit the *Culture Club* at Forest Glen School. Here are my observations:

The bell rings for lunch. Candace greets the students at the door with a warm smile and '*Hello, my friends.*' The earliest arrivals sit down and watch a video that Candace already has playing about the United Arab Emirates (UAE). I am amazed to count 35 little bodies by the time the day's presentation begins. A little boy named Aamir from the UAE is invited to the front. He is dressed in traditional clothing, the Kandura, and holds a duotang in his hand. Although he opens his duotang, he rarely uses it, except to show photographs to his audience. He discusses the national flag, the animals, the clothes, and food. There are many questions, and I am impressed by the depth of interest. Someone asks about the dates, and Aamir explains they are called Sahara dates and that they are delicious. Someone else asks about the language. Candace asks Aamir if he can teach them a word in Arabic. He obliges and teaches everyone how to say 'Hello.' Candace plays a video showcasing the landscapes. At one point, Aamir interjects, 'This used to be a desert.' Another student, Chris, who is also from the UAE adds, 'In 14 years it transformed from a desert to this!' The students, and we adults, are in awe of the pace of construction. Candace plays the national anthem of the UAE and asks the students if they would like to stand. The students stand in silence for Ishy Bilady, which translates to Long Live My Nation. Aamir answers a few more questions, and Candace plays a video of the national dance. Everyone, including Candace, is on their feet dancing. Aamir is thanked by everyone, and the meeting ends. Almost three dozen smiling faces disappear from the room, replete with those 'feel-good' neurotransmitters.

Following the meeting, the students returned to their classrooms to eat lunch, and Candace and I sat down for a chat. I asked if she would offer some advice to you. Here is her 'DO' list,

1. Listen to your students.
2. Let them be the leaders.
3. Start small and let it grow.

Her 'DON'T' list was fairly short,

1. Never make assumptions.

In addition to organizing the Culture Club, Candace also meets with the MLL in her office. It is in these moments that she is able to help mitigate traumas related to forced migration, as well as ease feelings of loneliness and homesickness. For example, during one such meeting, a young student conveyed that he missed the sand garden he had at home. Tending to his sand garden must have brought some measure of peace to him. It was not long before Candace had a small sand garden in her office.

Everyone benefits from the efforts of this committed teacher. Parents' anxiety is eased knowing that their children's anxiety is eased and that they are in very good hands at Forest Glen. Parent feedback on social media is a testament to that. The *Culture Club* serves as a catalyst for increased inclusivity back in the students' classrooms, prompting teachers to incorporate activities that acknowledge and honor the diverse backgrounds of their students. Seeing their students from an asset-based perspective is fundamental to their success. Additionally, the trusting relationships the students develop with Candace and, importantly, with each other are pivotal to engaging in higher learning back in their classrooms.

The members of the *Culture Club* are being prepared to navigate a world marked by differences, and they are eagerly enjoying every minute. Ultimately, Candace aims to establish a school community where every student and family feels heard, valued, and respected, leading to greater overall success and a sense of love and acceptance for everyone. As I left this little school, I couldn't help but ponder the magnitude of our jobs and how one person can so positively impact the trajectories of so many lives (nugget) (A. Bartlett, personal communication, November 27, 2023).

Culturally Responsive Teaching

As we move into culturally responsive teaching (CRT) and CRE, reflect upon Candace Douglass and Forest Glen School. CRT actively incorporates students' cultural backgrounds into the curriculum, thus making learning more relevant and relatable for them. Further, it cultivates a deeper understanding of different perspectives and encourages critical thinking because it connects the curriculum to real-world experiences. It is a way to diminish systemic biases within the educational system, including student evaluations, which are normed for the dominant culture, thereby providing a more equitable learning environment (nugget).

Teacher educator, critically acclaimed author, and pedagogical theorist Dr. Gloria Ladson-Billings (2014) describes CRT as a perspective that 'empowers students intellectually, socially, emotionally, and politically by using cultural referents to impart knowledge, skills, and attitudes.' She states that the gap between the culture of the home and that of the school can be closed by employing culturally relevant pedagogy. Dr. Ladson-Billings first introduced the concept of culturally relevant pedagogy in the 1990s.

We have chosen three former teachers who are now experts in the field of CRT and CRE: Geneva Gay (PhD), Zaretta Hammond, and Adeyemi Stembridge (PhD). The books, articles, and videos by these authors are a good place to begin a more comprehensive study of this topic.

Dr. Geneva Gay is a distinguished professor, author, speaker, and former classroom teacher. Among her publications is her influential book *Culturally Responsive Teaching: Theory, Research, and Practice* (2010). We are going to watch a video interview called *Culturally Responsive Teaching*,[10] accessible by following these steps:

1. Go to YouTube.
2. Search *'Culturally Responsive Teaching'* (Clint Born) Dr. Geneva Gay. It is 36:05 minutes long.

She advocates for a shift from the deficit mindset, from what our students can't do to what they can do. If the culture of the school is not in sync with the culture of a student, then the explanation of why a student isn't doing well should be addressed at the site of the clash.

Dr. Gay shares the following strategies for culturally responsive teachers.

1. Examine and revise, as possible, the curricula.
   There are three main types of curricula: the formal, which you are required to teach; the hidden, which you teach by how you interact with your students; and the symbolic, which relates to what/who is on display around the learning environment. Dr. Gay also mentions a fourth curriculum, the curriculum of the media. The messages that students receive through movies, TV, and music

videos are all influencing how students see themselves and their cultures. Teachers can intervene here as well, with more appropriate messages.

2. Care but in a manner that is dedicated and determined to find ways to leverage students' cultures to ensure they do not fail.

3. Understand and utilize the modes of communication of the students' cultures. For example, if a student's culture uses an oral form of communication versus the written form, then permitting the student to orate rather than write will give a better indication of what they can do. For students whose cultures use oral communication, communication through writing needs to be explicitly taught, but in the appropriate setting. So, be clear and precise about what you are assessing at that time.

4. Create an environment that reflects the diversity of society so that students see an acknowledgment of their culture and themselves. Attention should be given to physical, relational, and symbolic aspects of the learning environment.

5. Allow multiple options for learning. Members of some ethnic groups prefer to work in groups; others prefer to work alone.

6. Both the delivery of instruction and methods of feedback should be culture-sensitive. A student from a collectivist culture may be very uncomfortable with individual praise, especially if it is in front of the group they worked with.

7. Honor students' traditional means of assessment first. Then, transition students to the school's mode of assessment.

Zaretta Hammond (www.ready4rigor.com) is a former teacher and author of the book *Culturally Responsive Teaching and the Brain* (2015). She approaches the topic from the social neuroscience point of view, detailing how relationships reduce stress and allow for higher-order thinking. You can see a webinar of

Zaretta's called *Culturally Responsive Teaching and the Brain*[11] by following the steps:

1. Go to YouTube
2. Search 'Zaretta Hammond: *Culturally Responsive Teaching and the Brain Webinar*' by Corwin. It is 57:49 minutes long.

Zaretta states that a good launch point for teachers is the Cultural Index, first presented by Dr. Geert Hofstede (2010). Dr. Hofstede created several different continuums, one of which is individualism vs collectivism of different cultures around the globe. It assesses the extent to which individuals prioritize themselves over the group/community. The scale ranges from 0 to 100. A high score indicates a more individualistic culture where 'I' is prioritized over 'We.' Let's see where our countries rank.

Step 1: Google 'Hofstede Insights.'[12]
Step 2: Scroll to the bottom and select 'Compare Different Countries.'
Step 3: Select your country. A report follows below the data.

Canada and the USA both rank very high. In the video, Zaretta points out that the culture of origin (or ancestry) and the culture in which the student is being educated may differ widely on this continuum. If the culturally diverse learners are from collectivist cultures, the teacher can consider how to embed more collectivism into the classroom. Some might argue that students need to learn to be independent learners. In the webinar you watched, Zaretta states that since the collective is dependent on the individual doing their part, it also promotes independent learning. She adds that a collectivist environment within the classroom, coupled with a trusting relationship with the teacher, will better enable the students to build upon their current strengths to reach their full potential. The skills developed in a collectivist classroom align well with the 21st-century skills as detailed in the World Economic Forum. Our students will be required to work well with others (World Economic Forum, 2016).

Dr. Adeyemi Stembridge (https://www.dryemis.com/about) is the author of *Culturally Responsive Education in the Classroom: An Equity Framework for Pedagogy* (Stembridge, 2020). Originally, he was a high school English teacher. Now, he is a consultant and mentor to educators who are seeking strategies for closing achievement gaps and creating more equitable learning environments. Your next Brain Break is an example of CRT in an elementary school, specifically fourth grade.

You will view the process through the lens of the students, the teachers, and the coach, Dr. Stembridge. This is an authentic example of CRE done in one of his residencies. Please allow yourself time to watch it, rewind, and watch it again if needed.

Break Time #3D! Dr. Adeyemi Stembridge and CRE in Action

Watch the video: *What Are Culturally Responsive Education Teacher Residencies?*[13] or

1. Go to YouTube.
2. Search *'What Are Culturally Responsive Education Teacher Residencies?'* from the Centre for Strengthening the Teaching Profession (CSTP). It is 2 hours long, but fear not! The middle section is the actual CRE done in one of his residencies.

The video is a debrief of a professional learning experience put on by CSTP. It incorporates a residency program whereby Dr. Stembridge mentors staff on CRE. In the first 30 minutes, you are introduced to Dr. Stembridge and get an overview of the tenets of CRT. From the 00:30 to 1:06h mark is an authentic application of CRE in a grade 4 classroom. From the 1:06 to 2:00h mark is a panel discussion by administrators and teachers in another school who went through the residency program with Dr. Stembridge. We will focus on the 00:30 to 1:06h section; however, all of it is relevant to the topic. If you feel overwhelmed, that's okay. Take note of the commitment from staff and district, the time allotted for professional learning, and investment in the mentorship process made by the administration.

Part 1
00:00–00:30h

a. Summarize CRE:
b. What are the six themes of culturally responsive educa-
    tion (CRE) upon which you design learning experiences?
c. What are Dr. Stembridge's five guiding questions in no
    particular order?
d. Why is reflecting on the planning so important?
e. What do equity and pedagogy have to do with plan-
    ning for CRE?

Part 2
00:30 to 1:06h
We are including links to the resources mentioned in this
section

ReadWriteThink[14] by going to the URL 'www.
Readwritethink.org.'

Question Formulation Technique[15] by googling 'Right
Question Institute Question Formulation Technique.'

Interdisciplinary Read Alouds[16] by going to YouTube and
searching 'Interdisciplinary Learning Read Alouds.'

For this section, we are asking an open-ended question:

f. How does CRE, like the one showcased in the video,
    help to close equity gaps?

Part 3
1:06–2:00h
I found the rigor matrix, introduced by the middle school
instructional coach, Mark, particularly noteworthy. The
rigor matrix was used to help plan the lessons. Again, we
hear about the importance of planning lessons that incre-
mentally move students toward the deepest knowledge. By
charting Bloom's taxonomy with Webb's depth of knowledge, teachers can select what kind of thinking students
will need in a lesson. Once that is done, teachers can then
create better opportunities for students to use their cultural

identities to make connections between what they already know and what they are being taught. There are different rigor matrices depending on the subject matter. Simply do a Google search for 'Hess Cognitive Rigor Matrix for …' and select whatever course you wish. For example, there is one for ELA called the Hess Cognitive Rigor Matrix for ELA,[17] for which you can do a Google search.

In all likelihood, your classroom is more culturally diverse than the classrooms of 20 years ago. It behooves us to foster inclusive and enriching learning experiences for all of our students. Cultural humility and cultural competence are essential for effective communication with students, parents, and staff. Additionally, role modeling continuous self-reflection and a willingness to learn about different perspectives will nurture greater social awareness, empathy, and a growth mindset within our students, thus better preparing them for an increasingly globalized world.

Answers to Brain Breaks

Break Time #3A! Let's see how well you can shift from deficit thinking to asset thinking.

Deficit Thinking	Asset Thinking
Na-Moo is very uncomfortable.	Eye contact with superiors can be seen as disrespectful, thus Na-Moo is showing respect for her teacher and classmates.
Na-Moo's command of our language is not as good as I once thought.	In Asian communication, pausing indicates the listener is giving careful thought before responding. Respect for the speaker is being conveyed.
Na-Moo seems aloof or has a flat affect when speaking.	Koreans tend to keep a straight face when speaking. It's simply a cultural difference.
Na-Moo needs to be assessed by our School Team or Guidance Counselor.	Sometimes Koreans laugh when uncomfortable and smile when they have made a mistake. These are simply cultural differences.

Break Time #3B: Ethnocentrism vs. Cultural Relativism

Ethnocentrism	Cultural Relativism
It is wrong/cruel for a child to be fasting all day.	Maryem actually eats two meals a day, one 'power meal' before dawn and a large meal shared with family, friends, and neighbors after dusk.
Maryem is disengaged from everyone all day. It looks as though she has stopped caring.	Maryem enjoys the social times spent with family and friends during the evening feast. Furthermore, Maryem is learning about charity through her parents' contributions.

The holy month of Ramadan. This sacred time is based on the lunar cycle and so changes by about ten days each year. It is marked by fasting each day from dawn to dusk. However, a pre-dawn meal is eaten as well as a post-dusk meal. Children younger than 11 or 12 are not obligated to fast. For Maryem, this is her first year participating in the fast, so she is learning about self-discipline.

Break Time #3C! Your Cultural Humility

Your answers are personal to you.

Break Time #3D! Dr. Adeyemi Stembridge and CRE in Action

Part 1
00:00–00:30h

a. Summarize CRE:
    A method to close learning gaps in ways that do not marginalize any students over any others that actively enlist the students' identities as they relate to culture, race, ethnicity, gender, ability, etc. It allows students to draw on their identities to demonstrate competence.

b. What are the six themes of CRE upon which you design learning experiences?
    Vulnerability
    Cultural identity

Assets
Rigor
Engagement
Relationships

c. What are Dr. Stembridge's five guiding questions in no particular order?
What do we want students to understand?
What do we want students to feel?
What are the targets for rigor?
What are the indicators for engagement?
What are the opportunities to be responsive?

d. Why is reflecting on the planning so important?
It is important because in the reflection, we can see what part of our planning allowed for the student engagement that we saw.

e. What do equity and pedagogy have to do with planning for CRE?
The layered approach to CRE necessitates action from two intersecting fronts: equity and pedagogy. Equity: whom, Pedagogy: how.

00:30 to 1:06h

An open-ended question: How does CRE, like the one showcased in the video, help to close equity gaps?

f. As I think about this chapter, specifically the section on CRE, I consider the following:

Of the 16 21st-century skills (as defined by the World Economic Forum), about 12 were either required or could be improved upon in this project (World Economic Forum, 2016).

They are literacy, cultural literacy, critical thinking, creativity, communication, collaboration, curiosity, persistence, initiative, leadership, and social and cultural awareness.

Dr. Stembridge's six themes were incorporated in the following ways.

Vulnerability: of parents and students as they shared information.

Cultural identity: revealed through the interview with parents and discussions with the teacher.

Assets: due to the freedom students were allowed, they were no doubt able to showcase their assets and with guidance from the teacher, improve in other areas.

Rigor: students moved from closed questions to open questions to gain further insights into their families' themes. Persistence was key.

Engagement: high because it was deeply relevant to the students' own lives. However, by knowing the students well, teachers could (and did) set engagement traps for those students for whom they were concerned.

Relationships: student-student (peer reviews), student-teacher (sharing of interviews), and student-parent (interviews) all required tremendous honesty and trust.

In the video...

The classroom is culturally diverse.

Some students are refugees with sad histories.

The students seemed relaxed and bonded with other students and the teacher in conversations (dopamine, serotonin, oxytocin).

Students were engaged.

The project was cross-curricular, centered on the topic of *Theme*

Skills of the formal curriculum (as per Dr. Gay) were addressed, including listening, reading, and writing.

The project wasn't about culture but the topic of *Theme* incorporated the students' culture to make it more relatable.

The learning environment was full of respect for the students' cultures and empty of stereotypes (hidden curriculum).

Teachers gained a better understanding of their students as cultural beings by parental involvement via the interviews. Utilizing members of the community and parents is a central theme in CRE.

The teachers were flexible in their pedagogy. Teaching did not occur with the typical talk and chalk method. Daily monitoring allowed teachers to assess what the students were understanding and address what they were not understanding in a timely manner. This may have been done in a class, in a small group, or even in a one-on-one.

Rigor was evident as teachers worked to move students from what they could do to what they could not (yet) do. Students found that asking open-ended questions vs closed-ended questions yielded deeper, more detailed answers.

Students peer-reviewed. The collectivist nature of this activity has many benefits.

Students engaged in self-reflection, which fosters greater autonomy.

Students were reading from other authors (one student mentioned she was reading about Malala Yousafzai). By having publications from culturally diverse authors, students were able to view the world from different perspectives. It is up to the teacher to provide appropriate resources and minimize negative stereotypes from media (symbolic and media curriculum as per Dr. Gay)

Students experienced the power of the growth mindset (as opposed to a fixed mindset), and hard work can improve one's abilities.

Parents could engage in storytelling, the passing on of ancestral information via the answers they provided to their children.

Parents engaged in truly meaningful dialogue with their children.

1:06–2:00h

No questions asked.

Just food for thought.

Notes

1 https://www.youtube.com/watch?app=desktop&v=izmkRYbq2Sg.
2 https://www.youtube.com/watch?v=egw-iheD1Mc.
3 https://implicit.harvard.edu/implicit/takeatest.html.
4 https://implicit.harvard.edu/implicit/langchoice/canada.html.
5 https://ssrce.ca/wp-content/uploads/2012/08/Bias-Evaluation-Instrument-09092015.pdf.
6 https://culturalatlas.sbs.com.au/south-korean-culture/south-korean-culture-communication.
7 https://www.youtube.com/watch?v=wlyS4zrklww&t=248s.
8 https://www.unrefugees.org/news/what-to-know-about-ramadan-and-how-refugees-celebrate/#:~:text=A%20few%20ways%20Muslims%20celebrate,abstain%20from%20food%20and%20drink.
9 https://smho-smso.ca/wp-content/uploads/2022/11/Cultural-humility-tool-for-school-staff.pdf.
10 https://www.youtube.com/watch?v=6ua6YPZ_fdk.
11 https://www.youtube.com/watch?v=O2kzbH7ZWGg&t=2635s.
12 https://www.hofstede-insights.com/.
13 https://www.youtube.com/watch?v=t8yUUelzrN0&t=5764s.
14 https://www.readwritethink.org/.
15 https://rightquestion.org/what-is-the-qft/.
16 https://www.youtube.com/@educ329interdisciplinaryle7.
17 https://static.pdesas.org/content/documents/M1-Slide_22_DOK_Hess_Cognitive_Rigor.pdf.

Suggested Resources

Books

Gay, G. (2018). *Culturally responsive teaching: Theory, research, and practice.* Teacher's College Press.

Hammond, Z. (2015). *Culturally responsive teaching and the brain: Promoting authentic engagement and rigor among culturally and linguistically diverse students.* Corwin.

Hofstede, G., Hofstede, G. J., & Minkov, M. (2010). *Cultures and organizations: Software of the mind.* McGraw-Hill Education.

Ladson-Billings, Gloria. (2009). *The dreamkeepers: Successful teachers of African American children; Crossing over to Canaan: The journey of new teachers in diverse classrooms; Beyond the big house: African American educators on teacher education.* Wiley.

Stembridge, A. (2023). *Brilliant teaching: Using culture and artful thinking to close equity gaps.* Jossey-Bass, a Wiley brand.

Valencia, Richard (1997). *The evolution of deficit thinking: Educational thought and practice.* Falmer Press.

Websites

♦ YouTube show Ahlan Simsim and resources from the makers of SesameWorkshop.org (https://ahlansimsim.org/)

♦ Lesson plans and tool kit (https://www.safeatschool.ca/resources/resources-on-equity-and-inclusion/racism/tool-kits-and-activities)

♦ https://asmonsoft.com

♦ https://bookako.com

♦ https://www.nicabm.com

Canadian Content

♦ Culturally relevant pedagogy – Inclusion Canada (https://www.inclusioncanada.net/culturallyrelevantpedagogy.html)

♦ Culturally relevant teaching | Fall 2019 | Education Canada magazine (https://www.edcan.ca/magazine/fall-2019/)

♦ Capacity building series – Culturally responsive pedagogy (https://www2.yrdsb.ca/sites/default/files/migrate/files/cbs_responsivepedagogy.pdf)

♦ Culturally responsive pedagogy: A Canadian perspective | *Journal of Higher Education Policy and Leadership Studies* (https://johepal.com/article-1-92-en.pdf)

♦ Equity and inclusion for all: Culturally responsive teaching and assessment pedagogy (https://heartandart.ca/honouring-student-identity-culturally-responsive-teaching-and-assessment-pedagogy-for-building-an-equitable-and-inclusive-classroom-for-all/)

- Elementary classroom: An integrated approach to culturally responsive pedagogy (https://teslcanadajournal.ca/index.php/tesl/article/view/1407/1235)

Immigrants and Refugees

- Immigrants and refugees as funds of knowledge (https://www.tandfonline.com/doi/epdf/10.1080/01434632.2023.2170389?needAccess=true)

CRT

- Culturally responsive teaching for multilingual learners: Tools for equity (https://www.youtube.com/watch?v=CVNiKvcKZXg)
- Culturally responsive teaching guide ten examples (https://pce.sandiego.edu/culturally-responsive-teaching-guide-10-examples/#:~:text=Culturally%20responsive%20teaching%20is%20%E2%80%9Ca,cultural%20place%20in%20the%20world)
- Why our trauma-informed teaching must be more culturally responsive | EdSurge news (https://www.edsurge.com/news/2021-10-08-why-our-trauma-informed-teaching-must-be-more-culturally-responsive)
- A guide to culturally responsive teaching and resources (https://www.routledge.com/blog/article/a-guide-to-culturally-responsive-teaching-and-resources)

Deficit Thinking

- The deficit model is harming your students | Edutopia (https://www.edutopia.org/blog/deficit/-model-is-harming-students-janice-lambardi)
- Dismantling contemporary deficit thinking: Educational thought and practice (https://www.researchgate.net/publication/287243813_Dismantling_Contemporary_Deficit_Thinking_Educational_Thought_and_Practice)

For Teacher Training/Preparation

◆ Building capacity for inclusive teaching: Policies and practices to Prepare All Teachers for diversity and inclusion | OECD education working papers (https://www.oecd-ilibrary.org/docserver/57fe6a38-en.pdf?expires=1702930532&id=id&accname=guest&checksum=FD6AFFD0003A8B1CFB9164F662ABE308)

◆ Cultural bias in assessment: Can creativity assessment help? (https://uscaseps.org/wp-content/uploads/2020/07/standardized-testing.pdf)

◆ Implicit bias tests – Why every teacher should take a few (https://www.weareteachers.com/implicit-bias-tests/)

◆ Implicit bias | Inclusive teaching | Teaching guides | Teaching commons | DePaul University, Chicago (https://resources.depaul.edu/teaching-commons/teaching-guides/inclusive-teaching/Pages/implicit-bias.aspx)

◆ https://www.gse.harvard.edu/ideas/usable-knowledge/17/04/responding-bias-school

References

Bushnell, Lauren. (2021, April). *Educational disparities among racial and ethnic minority youth in the United States*. Ballard Brief. www.ballardbrief.org

Ciuffetelli Parker, D., & Conversano, P. (2021). Narratives of systemic barriers and accessibility: Poverty, equity, diversity, inclusion, and the call for a post-pandemic new normal. *Frontiers in Education, 6*, 704663. https://doi.org/10.3389/feduc.2021.704663

Covey, S. M. R., & Merrill, R. R. (2018). *The speed of trust: The one thing that changes everything*. Free Press.

Doucet, A. (2019). *Teaching life: Our calling, our choices, our challenges*. Routledge.

Glaser, J. E. (2014). *Conversational intelligence: How great leaders build trust and get extraordinary results*. Bibliomotion, Inc.

Jupia Consultants Inc. (2023). (rep.). *Profile of the immigrant and non-permanent resident population in Greater Moncton (2021 census)*, 2021 Census, City of Moncton.

Kaiser, B., & Rasminsky, J. S. (2020). Valuing diversity: Developing a deeper understanding of all young children's behavior. *NAEYC*. https://www.naeyc.org/resources/pubs/tyc/dec2019/valuing-diversity-developing-understanding-behavior

Kreskow, Kelly. (2013). Overrepresentation of minorities in special education. Education Masters. Paper 257.

Ladson-Billings, Gloria. (2014). Culturally relevant pedagogy 2.0: A.k.a. the remix. *Harvard Educational Review*, *84*(1), 74–84.

McBrien, J. (2022), Social and emotional learning (SEL) of newcomer and refugee students: Beliefs, practices and implications for policies across OECD countries. *OECD Education Working Papers*, No. 266, (pp. 12–15), OECD Publishing, Paris.

Patton Davis, L., & Museus, S. D. (2019). What is deficit thinking? An analysis of conceptualizations of deficit …. *Currents*. https://quod.lib.umich.edu/c/currents/17387731.0001.110?view=text;rgn=main

Pit-ten Cate, Ineke M., & Glock, Sabine. (2018). Teacher expectations concerning students with immigrant backgrounds or special educational needs. *Educational Research and Evaluation*, *24*(3–5), 277–294. https://doi.org/10.1080/13803611.2018.1550839

Singh, S. (1970, January 1). Overrepresentation of immigrants in special education. A grounded theory study on the case of Austria. *pedocs*. https://www.pedocs.de/frontdoor.php?source_opus=21197

Stembridge, A. (2020). *Culturally responsive education in the classroom: An equity framework for pedagogy*. Corwin.

Tervalon, M., & Murray-García, J. (1998). Cultural humility versus cultural competence: A critical distinction in defining physician training outcomes in multicultural education. *Journal of Health Care for the Poor and Underserved*, *9*(2), 117–125. Project MUSE, https://doi.org/10.1353/hpu.2010.0233

Valencia, R. R. (2010). *Dismantling contemporary deficit thinking: Educational thought and practice* (1st ed.). Routledge. https://doi.org/10.4324/9780203853214

World Economic Forum. (2016, March 10). *Ten 21st-century skills every student needs*. https://www.weforum.org/agenda/2016/03/21st-century-skills-future-jobs-students/

4

Safety and Predictability

One of the tenets of a trauma-informed school is 'safety and predictability.' Physical and psychological safety allows the engagement of the prefrontal cortex. Remember, the prefrontal cortex is the rational part of students' brains that may be silenced by the stress response. Safety and predictability are achieved by a warm, attentive, and empathic approach to students, acknowledging trauma triggers, predictable classroom procedures, and curriculum adaptations to meet individual needs (Rishel et al., 2019).

Attachment

We discussed Bowlby's Attachment Theory in Chapter 2. We know that building trust and creating authentic connections and relationships with our students will result in the behavioral changes that we are looking for (Wyatt & Oliver, 2016). For example, responding to students with soothing words can provide feelings of safety, security, and hope, while positive, caring, supportive relationships can be a buffer against the effects of trauma (Chafouleas et al., 2019). Do not underestimate the power of healthy attachments between teachers and students. Deep learning cannot happen without it.

Attachment has a foundation in biology because it can actually impact brain development. Warm and supportive relationships positively impact neural development, allowing for better

DOI: 10.4324/9781032707945-7

emotional regulation (Blakemore, 2018). However, we know that not all attachments are secure. Insecure attachments may result in other behaviors, such as clinginess, hostility, attention-seeking, and highly anxious responses to situations (Webber, 2017). As Zaretta Hammond stated in the Chapter 3 video, if a student is not able to self-regulate, they can stay in a state of hyper-arousal which interferes with their problem-solving ability, concentration, and ability to ask for help (Hammond, 2018; Webber, 2017).

In childhood, empathy is promoted by secure attachments with the caregiver and is hindered by insecure ones. Empathy is important in interpersonal relationships later in life (Xu et al., 2022). How important is empathy in your classroom? Empathy was used as a factor in a study assessing what happens when teachers are educated about the effects of disrupted attachments. In that study, the teachers felt the training enabled them to reflect on the behaviors of their students before responding. As a result, the investigators determined that empathy plays an important role in developing healthy teacher-student relationships in part because it enables the teachers to reframe their students' difficult classroom behaviors (Little & Maunder, 2022). Teacher stress is reduced (nugget)!

In Chapter 3, we introduced oxytocin. Remember, it is a hormone that is released in one's brain during the bonds formed in caring, warm, and trusting relationships with others (Reilly & Gunnar, 2019). This hormone reduces cortisol levels during times of stress (Uvnas-Moberg & Petersson, 2005); thus, we see the link between the hormone and the regulation of the stress response by social attachment (Reilly & Gunnar, 2019).

One day, I was telling a colleague, Dr. Deanna O'Donnell, about this book. At the time, I was writing Chapter 3. She related to me a 'teachable moment' she had just had with some of her students. Her period 1 chemistry students had just finished writing a test that had caused them stress. Her period 2 students were waiting outside to write the same test. Naturally, the first-period students conveyed their thoughts about the test to the second-period students. The second-period students then entered the room in a state of panic and wrote (unsuccessfully) the same test. The chemistry was clear. The only thing needed to cause oxytocin to be secreted is another person, so when the first-period students saw friends waiting in the hallway, their oxytocin levels surged, and they, in a manner of speaking, infected period 2 students with their stress. While releasing oxytocin helped reduce cortisol levels (Li et al., 2019) in the period 1 students, the cortisol levels in the period 2 students rose. Deanna added that she had seen anxiety expressed as this equation:

anxiety = stressor / one's perception of how they can handle stress

She stated that many people focus on the numerator, the stressor, but should instead focus on the denominator, their perception of how they can handle it. Deanna suggested this video by Stanford psychologist Kelly McGonigal to help you understand the role of oxytocin called *How to Make Stress Your Best Friend (Condensed Talk)*.[1] Simply search for it on YouTube.

(Dr. Deanna O'Donnell, personal communication with author Alison Bartlett, November 17, 2023).

Dr. William Glasser was an American psychiatrist who developed therapeutic approaches according to what he called 'Choice Theory.' He believed that after food and shelter, everyone needs to fulfill four psychological needs to be healthy. In Glasser's opinion, 'love, acceptance, and belonging' are the main psychological needs, while 'competence' is the second most important need. In addition, all individuals require 'fun' and 'freedom' in their lives (Glasser, 2001). This theory could be seen at work in the CRT section of Chapter 3. So, with Glasser's theory in mind, establishing a learning environment of acceptance and belonging as a means to circumvent stress responses in our students should be at the top of our 'to-do' list. While physical safety can be accomplished by ensuring the school environment meets the needs of the staff and the students, psychological safety includes understanding the students' trauma history, their triggers at school, and the skills they need to be taught to regulate their emotions (Parker, 2020).

Break Time #4A! Safety and Predictability in Your Classroom and School.

Reflect upon your classroom and school. What are you/your staff doing that promotes safety and predictability?

	Classroom	School

Regular routines that are visible to students.

Explicit lessons about interpersonal skills and emotional regulation.

Explicit lessons about resilience.

Genuinely warm, welcoming, and accepting environment for *all* students.

Students' cultures and identities are reflected in the school environment, including resources.

Learning opportunities connect to families' histories and language.

Learning opportunities are accessible, challenging, and inspiring according to their strengths.

Safe spaces for students to ask questions and express their interests, values, perspectives, learning strengths, and challenges.

A supervised, non-punitive chill-out space where students can metabolize cortisol.

Reflective listening is practiced when communicating with students, parents, and other staff.

Regular feedback to parents, including the positive.

Develop a collaborative and welcoming environment for parents and guardians to contribute to their children's education.

Respectful relations among staff (role modeling).

Teachers collaborate with their support staff, teachers, and school-based planning teams, as well as parents to identify the learning needs and strengths of the students.

(nugget)

Mirror Neurons

Do teachers really 'create the climate of the classroom'? The discovery and observation of mirror neurons can help us answer this question. Most of us are familiar with the neurons in our brains that mimic the *actions* of others. For example, when someone yawns while we are looking at them, we automatically yawn. Interestingly, researchers have discovered neurons that mimic the *emotions* of others as well. A study used brain imaging to observe the activity of neurons when individuals observed the emotion of disgust. The brains of people were imaged using an MRI as they inhaled noxious odors such as butyric acid, which smells like rotten butter. As individuals observed the wrinkling of the faces of the people experiencing disgust, they not only wrinkled their faces in response but *felt* disgusted. So, *feeling* disgusted and *watching* someone else look disgusted activated the same neurons in the brain (Wicker et al., 2003).

The discovery of these amazing neurons validates the concept that teachers create the climate of the classroom. In other words, if you have feelings of disapproval, judgment, annoyance, and frustration in the classroom, the same emotions are felt by your students. On the other hand, compassion, acceptance, trust, optimism, and belief in your students' abilities are also felt by students. Worse, your feelings about a student could impact how other students feel about them (nugget).

Identifying and Removing Triggers

As described in Chapter 1, when a student perceives a physical or psychological threat, their stress response is triggered, leading to a variety of behaviors that interfere with learning in the classroom. Students who have ACEs are more likely to perceive threats in their environment, including the school environment.

From the video *Trauma and the Incredible Hulk*, if a student has already been triggered, all you can do is provide a safe 'chill-out' space for them to metabolize their cortisol. But if they haven't yet been triggered, you can remove specific things that a child perceives as threatening. What might they be? Well, triggers are unique to each child and really depend on their previous experiences and their individual sensitivity to internal and external stimuli. So, careful observations and non-threatening communication with the student may help you identify them. You will then be able to modify your classroom or school to help them feel safer.

Dr. Stuart Shanker has identified five domains of triggers to be aware of. The extensive and thorough list is called the Self-Reg Framework: The Five Domains of Stress[2] (published with permission from Dr. Shanker and The MEHRIT Centre).

1. Google 'self-reg.ca.'
2. Go to the search bar and type in 'Five Domains.'
3. Click on the image of the two toddlers playing.

Dr. Shanker categorizes potential triggers into biological, social, emotional, prosocial, and cognitive. You can investigate them individually by clicking on each domain (links are in red) (Figure 4.1)

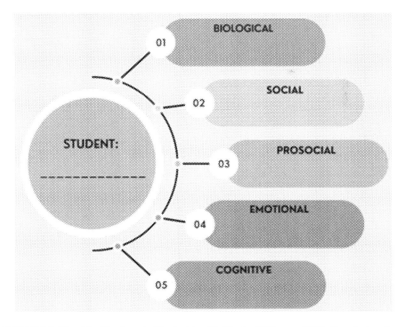

FIGURE 4.1 Chart for Teachers to Use to Identify Student Triggers (With Permission from the MEHRIT)

is an information sheet that you can print out and fill in when assessing a student's triggers.

Is it always possible to identify triggers? Let's think back to 'Psychology 101' and revisit Pavlov's observations of salivating dogs. Ivan Petrovich Pavlov was a Russian neurologist and physiologist who lived in the late 1800s/early 1900s. He did groundbreaking research, discovering what we know as Classical Conditioning. Pavlov noticed the dogs he observed in his laboratory automatically salivated, which was an unconscious response whenever they saw food. The researcher then paired the introduction of food with the ringing of a bell; the dogs learned to associate the bell with food. This was the birth of Classical Conditioning since when Pavlov rang the bell without showing the dogs food, the dogs salivated anyway. In other words, they associated food with the ringing of the bell. The bell was labeled a 'conditioned stimulus'; the dogs salivating when associating the bell with food is a 'conditioned response.' So, do you think it is always possible to know what the trigger is? Sometimes, a student's amygdala senses a threat that may be a conditioned stimulus. In this case, they are associating something in their environment with a past threat that may not be consciously associated with the past experience. As a result, students may exhibit the FFFF responses without recognizing a specific trigger.

So, they may or may not be able to tell you what has triggered them. In this case, we can observe them and coach students to notice signs that they are becoming dysregulated and provide them with the opportunity to use the strategies presented in this and the next chapter to activate their PNS, which will calm their stress response. Remember that children's responses are unique to their personalities and experiences. Let's review from Chapter 1, the effects of activation of the stress response by the Sympathetic Nervous System: unable to concentrate, tense muscles, dilated pupils, crying, shaky, sweaty, fleeing the situation/ room, irritability, anger/violent, increased heartbeat, rapid shallow breathing, unable to articulate. Reflect on this chapter: what did you know, what did you learn, and how can you implement your knowledge to provide a safe and predictable learning environment for your students?

Answers to Brain Breaks

Break Time #4A! Safety and Predictability in Your Classroom and School.

Reflect upon your classroom and school. What are you/your staff doing that promotes safety and predictability?

We hope that after completing this book and its activities and brain breaks, you know what you and your staff can/should do to ensure that the stress responses of your traumatized students are not triggered, or if they are, that you have responded appropriately.

	Classroom	*School*
Regular routines that are visible to students	✔	✔
Explicit lessons about interpersonal skills and emotional regulation	✔	
Explicit lessons about resilience	✔	
Genuinely warm, welcoming, and accepting environment for *all* students	✔	✔
Students' cultures and identities are reflected in the school environment, including resources	✔	✔
Learning opportunities connect to families' histories and language	✔	
Learning opportunities are accessible, challenging, and inspiring according to their strengths	✔	
Safe spaces for students to ask questions, express their interests, values, perspectives, learning strengths and challenges	✔	✔
A supervised, non-punitive chill-out space where students can metabolize cortisol	✔	✔
Reflective listening is practiced when communicating with students, parents, and other staff	✔	✔
Regular feedback to parents, including the positive	✔	

	Classroom	School
Develop a collaborative and welcoming environment for parents and guardians to contribute to their child's education	✔	✔
Respectful relations among staff (role modeling)	✔	✔
Teachers collaborate with their support staff, teachers, school-based planning teams, as well as parents to identify the learning needs and strengths of the students	✔	✔

Notes

1 https://www.youtube.com/watch?v=RcGyVTAoXEU.
2 https://self-reg.ca/self-reg-framework-5-domains-stress/.

References

Blakemore, S. J. (2018). *Inventing ourselves: The secret life of the teenage brain.* Transworld Publishers.

Chafouleas, S. M., Koriakin, T. A., Roundfield, K. D., & Overstreet, S. (2019). Addressing childhood trauma in school settings: A framework for evidence-based practice. *School Mental Health, 11*(1), 40–53.

Glasser, W. (2001). *Choice theory: A new psychology of personal freedom.* HarperPerennial.

Hammond, Z. (2018). *Culturally responsive teaching and the brain webinar.* Corwin. https://www.youtube.com/watch?v=O2kzbH7ZWGg&t=2635s

Li, Y., Hassett, A. L., & Seng, J. S. (2019). Exploring the mutual regulation between oxytocin and cortisol as a marker of resilience. *Archives of Psychiatric Nursing, 33*(2), 164. https://doi.org/10.1016/j.apnu.2018.11.008

Little, S. & Maunder, R. (2022). Training secondary school teachers on early attachment trauma and adolescent brain development: Impact on empathy. *Educational Studies*, *48* (4), 508–512.

Parker, R. (2020). 'One size does not fit all': Engaging students who have experienced trauma. *Issues in Educational Research*, *30*(1), 245–259.

Reilly, E., Gunnar, M. (2019). Neglect, HPA axis reactivity, and development. *International Journal of Developmental Neuroscience*, *78*, 100–108. doi: https://doi.org/10.1016/j.ijdevneu.2019.07.010. Epub 2019 Jul 30. PMID: 31374220.

Rishel, C., Tabone, J., Hartnett, H., Szafran, K. (2019). Trauma-informed elementary schools: Evaluation of school-based early intervention for young children, *Children & Schools*, *41*(4), 239–248. https://doi.org/10.1093/cs/cdz017

Uvnas-Moberg, K., & Petersson, M. (2005). Oxytocin, ein Vermittler von Antistress, Wohlbefinden, sozialer Interaktion, Wachstum und Heilung [Oxytocin, a mediator of anti-stress, well-being, social interaction, growth and healing]. *Zeitschrift fur Psychosomatische Medizin und Psychotherapie*, *51*(1), 57–80. https://doi.org/10.13109/zptm.2005.51.1.57

Webber, L. (2017). A school's journey in creating a relational environment which supports attachment and emotional security. *Emotional and Behavioural Difficulties*, *22*(4), 317–331.

Wicker, B., Keysers, C., Plailly, J., Royet, J. P., Gallese, V., & Rizzolatti, G. (2003). Both of us disgusted in my insula: The common neural basis of seeing and feeling disgust. *Neuron*, *40*(3), 655–664. https://doi.org/10.1016/s0896-6273(03)00679-2

Wyatt, Z., & Oliver, L. (2016). Y-change: Young people as experts and collaborators. *Advances in Social Work and Welfare Education*, *18*(1), 121–126. View at Google Scholar

Xu, X., Liu, Z., Gong, S., & Wu, Y. (2022). The relationship between empathy and attachment in children and adolescents: Three-level meta-analyses. *International Journal of Environmental Research and Public Health*, *19*(3). https://doi.org/10.3390/ijerph19031391

5

Cognitive-Behavioral Theory

Now that you have an understanding of a trauma-informed school environment, it is time to delve into the 'how-to' for elementary school educators. Approaches that have proven to be highly effective in promoting emotional resilience at school include aspects of Cognitive-Behavioral Theory or CBT. CBT is a psychological framework that uses the connection between thoughts, feelings, and behaviors to explain students' emotional, cognitive, and behavioral responses to situations at school. As teachers learn and explore the theories and techniques related to this highly effective approach, insight, understanding, and empathy for students' perspectives and reactions will emerge. Strategies to promote emotional self-regulation and ways to recognize and challenge unhealthy thinking patterns for both your students and yourself will result. As you continue reading, you will learn concrete, usable, and adaptable strategies to employ in your classrooms, contributing to adaptable and resilient learners.

What Is Cognitive-Behavioral Theory?

Developed in the 1960s and 1970s by Dr. Aaron Beck, CBT is the most commonly used theory to improve anxiety and depressive symptoms in the world. It is based on the idea that thoughts influence feelings, feelings affect behaviors, and behaviors affect thoughts and feelings. According to the model, two people in the

DOI: 10.4324/9781032707945-8

same situation may feel differently depending on what they are thinking (Figure 5.1).

As teachers, we can teach students to recognize the relationship between thoughts, feelings, and behaviors when they begin to have feelings of distress. In other words, we can explain the types of unhelpful thoughts that cause negative feelings and teach them skills to rationalize their thoughts. Alternatively, we can teach and encourage students to explore behaviors that will engage their parasympathetic, 'rest and digest' nervous systems. This can be taught to the class or can be done on a one-on-one basis with the student and teacher or with the counselor and teacher.

Dr. Beck determined that patients who were experiencing mental health challenges were engaging in 'automatic thoughts' that included attitudes regarding themselves, others, and the future. He associated his patients' negative, automatic thoughts with the perpetuation of their poor mental health. Beck stated that individuals have a system of beliefs that are triggered by events and situations. When there is a misinterpretation of a situation by automatic thoughts or a system of beliefs, students feel distressed. Unhelpful thoughts can be challenged and replaced with more rational ones as irrational beliefs are identified. More accurate thoughts result in more positive feelings, reducing feelings of distress (Beck, 2019). Essentially, the theory is based on the idea that the triad of thoughts, feelings, and behaviors are interactive and can influence one another (Esther et al., 2020). Before reading further, let's see what this looks like. If you teach

FIGURE 5.1 Diagram Relating Thoughts, Feelings, Behaviors with Arrows

grades 1–3, here is a useful YouTube video called *Story Time with Lynn. Ninjas Know the CBT Triangle.*[1] Follow the steps:

1. Go to YouTube.
2. Search for '*Story Time with Lynn. Ninjas Know the CBT Triangle.*'

If you teach grades 3–6, check out the YouTube video called *The CBT Triangle – SEL Sketches.*[2] Follow these steps:

1. Go to YouTube.
2. Search for '*The CBT Triangle – SEL Sketches*' (it is done by SEL Sketches).

CBT has taken on many reiterations since the 1960s. Using the concept behind the triad of thoughts, feelings, and behaviors, we can teach skills to all elementary students to help them regulate their emotions. Of course, as educators, we also need to use the same concepts to regulate ourselves. This promotes 'co-regulation,' creating an environment in which students are provided a psychologically safe space to engage their 'rest and digest' system (nugget).

How Does CBT Work?

We can teach students that thoughts, feelings, and behaviors are interrelated, and we can teach them how to recognize their emotions. Additionally, they can be taught how to identify whether or not their thoughts regarding situations are rational by helping students look for evidence that their thoughts are accurate while challenging distorted cognitions that cause the students distress. Muscle relaxation (behavior) and using one's senses to calm a student's stress response can be demonstrated, allowing them to think more rationally (Baweja et al., 2016). Specific behavioral strategies may include manipulatives, noise-canceling headphones, weighted blankets, coloring, drawing, painting, sipping cold water, or calm music (Santiago et al., 2018). As students master the skills of CBT, they will be more likely to regulate their emotions, which will result in the ability to engage in learning, better interpersonal skills, and enhanced feelings of competency and autonomy.

Individuals have a system of beliefs triggered by events and situations. When there is a misinterpretation of a situation by automatic thoughts or a system of beliefs, students' functioning will be hindered. As maladaptive beliefs are identified, self-defeating thoughts can be challenged, replacing unhelpful thoughts with rational ones. Teachers can coach their students to recognize and challenge automatic negative thoughts, changing the meaning of pre-existing beliefs. As a result, more accurate thoughts cause more positive feelings, thereby regulating the HPA axis, which will enable higher-order thinking like problem-solving, and attention, as well as prosocial behaviors (Reilly & Gunnar, 2019). Teachers can certainly teach these basic approaches in the classroom.

Students who have been traumatized are more likely to perceive threats in their environment. As their HPA axis is triggered, the stress response results in a fight, flight, freeze, or fawn response (FFFF). Remember Figure 1.6 from Chapter 1? As cortisol and adrenaline increase, the student's quality of judgment/rational thinking declines.

CBT: Body→Brain

When the stress hormones have hijacked the thinking part of the brain, and the student has 'hulked out,' there is nothing you can do other than provide a safe space to 'chill out' while they metabolize their cortisol. Identifying and challenging one's thoughts is not possible at that moment. So, what is possible? The student can use the concept of the CBT triad to engage in behaviors that can change their feelings. They are activating their Parasympathetic Nervous System, or 'rest and digest' nervous system. We will refer to this as the body→brain, body to brain, or more simply, the body-brain approach. We are being deliberate about the direction of the arrow, as you will see.

The purpose of body-brain emotional regulation is to *calm* the Sympathetic Nervous System and engage the Parasympathetic Nervous System so that the thinking part of the brain can be accessed. There are two benefits to this approach. The first is you are teaching the valuable life skill of self-regulation. Second, you can all get back to the job at hand, the lesson/task/activity.

Sensory and physical activities (behaviors) help to ground students during a stress response by bringing their sensations into awareness and activating the Parasympathetic Nervous System. As students begin to feel safe, they can engage the rational prefrontal cortex (PFC) and then recognize the thoughts that preceded and precipitated their emotional response. When students can express their feelings by appropriate physical means, they lower their stress in the classroom and thus reduce disruptive behaviors (Levine, 2010).

Childhood trauma is usually not processed in the brain's PFC, where speech is processed, but early trauma may be processed in physical ways such as movement, drawing, and painting, and, as Banks and Meyer (2017) reveal in their study, sand play. Physical activities can be provided for the students to process their trauma rather than acting out their feelings in an aggressive manner. Specifically, they used sand play, movement, and the manipulation of sensory items with the students, leading to a reduction in aggressive classroom behaviors. In other words, safe and appropriate outlets for the energy that was produced during the stress response were made available to the students (nugget).

Setting up your classroom to be body-brain friendly would involve gathering and purchasing materials and setting up an area where students can take time to regulate their emotions, as Mrs. Jackson had in our Chapter 1 example. Hands-on activities can be used with the entire class or individual students. For example, you could begin each day/period with an activity to ground students in the here and now to prepare them for learning. If a student, like Kelly, is experiencing emotional dysregulation, you can invite them to engage in self-chosen activities in a quiet area in your classroom. You will be creating a learning environment that is both safe and predictable. Figure 5.2 provides some ideas for your students to try.

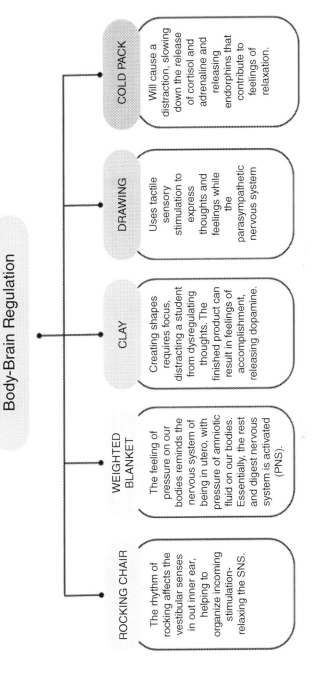

FIGURE 5.2 Examples of Brain-Body Regulation Strategies

Tactile and sensory interventions work differently for every child. A body-brain activity that is calming for one student may be stimulating for another. You'll need to observe and check in with students to get to know which tools assist them with emotional regulation. At this point, we ask that you remind yourself of images 1.6 and 1.7 in Chapter 1 to compare and contrast the graphs showing the beneficial effects of body-brain interventions.

Here is a little chart for collecting information to help you discover the activities, people, and strategies that support an individual student's emotional regulation. It would be useful to provide this to a supply teacher or during a conference regarding the student (Figure 5.3).

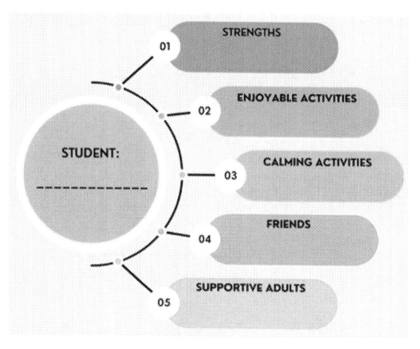

FIGURE 5.3 Chart to Organize Emotional Regulation Strategies for Specific Students

Social-Emotional Learning (SEL) Resources for You and Your Students

Some more types of manipulatives and activities to calm a student's SNS can be found in the 5-4-3-2-1 Method: A Grounding Exercise to Manage Anxiety.[3]

1. Go to YouTube.
2. Search for: *'The 5-4-3-2-1 Method: A Grounding Exercise to Manage Anxiety'* by The Partnership in Education.

   ◆ Let's have a look at a free, downloadable worksheet that can help your students identify their feelings as well as labels for their emotions at Where Do I Feel?[4] Simply

1. Do a Google search for 'Therapist Aid.'
2. In the search bar, type 'Where Do I Feel?'

Take a few moments, when you have time, to look through this website. There is a wide variety of topics which you can filter by age group.

◆ A valuable resource for lower elementary students is at Sesame Workshop, I notice, I Feel, I Can.[5] Or complete the following steps.

1. Do a Google search for 'Sesame Workshop.'
2. In the search bar, type in 'I Notice, I Feel, I Can.'
3. You will see three icons with the same title. One is an interactive game; one is a video; one is a worksheet that can accompany the video.

◆ The following can be used in all levels of elementary school. Which wheel you select will depend on the grade level of your students, called The Best Emotion Wheel.[6]

1. Do a Google search for 'Kairos Heros of Time.'
2. Click on 'Free Resources.'
3. Select 'Emotions Wheel.'

Regardless of how you access the page, you will have to provide your email address and then select 'download.' Underneath the picture of the wheels, click 'download.' You will see the three wheels. Select the one that best fits your students.

Flow

Another body-brain strategy for educators to be aware of to contribute to a trauma-informed school environment is the concept of 'flow.' Positive psychologist Mihály Csíkszentmihályi (2003) describes flow as a state of complete immersion in an activity.

Think of times when you are engaged in an activity with complete focus; you may have feelings of contentment, accomplishment, and/or joy. You wish to continue the activity to improve your skills and/or to work toward a finished product. Activities that lead to flow are different for everyone. For example, someone may lose track of time and become completely immersed in a sewing project, while someone else may experience flow when dancing. Other activities that commonly result in flow include painting, drawing, knitting, writing, sports, woodworking, playing an instrument, and gardening. Research reveals that there is also an increase in the activity of dopamine, which we introduced in Chapter 3. Remember, it is a brain chemical involved in pleasure and motivation. It is at work when people are engaged in flow (Örjan de Manzano et al., 2013). The key to obtaining this state of being is that an activity needs to be challenging enough to have to pay attention to but not so challenging that it causes anxiety and frustration (nugget). The activity should not be boring, nor should it require skills the students don't yet have (Figure 5.4).

FIGURE 5.4 Diagram Relating Thoughts, Feelings, Behaviors with Arrows

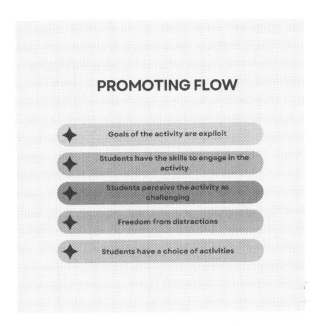

FIGURE 5.5 Ways to Promote 'Flow' with Students at School

Using the behaviors-feelings-thoughts triad, flow would be a body-brain activity that could regulate one's emotions by calming the SNS. So, how can we create environments at school to help our students to experience flow? (Figure 5.5).

Reflective Listening

Following a situation or event in which a student uses body-brain strategies to calm their stress response, reflective listening can provide an opportunity for the child to clarify their thoughts and explore their feelings regarding a situation. This involves paying close attention to the content and feelings that the student is expressing. Reflective listening is hearing and understanding, and then letting your student know that they are being heard and understood (Arnold, 2014). This requires you to focus solely on the student's body language and what they are saying.

This type of listening involves the following:

1. Hearing what the student is saying verbally and non-verbally from their perspective. This requires the suspension of judgment and personal perspectives while curiously listening for meaning.

2. Responding to the child with a description of what they have told you. The response may include content, feelings, and meaning of what you understood.
3. Providing an opportunity for the student to clarify that what you are reflecting back to them is in fact, what they mean. This is important.

For a student to communicate their thoughts, perspectives, and feelings, they need to trust the listener and to feel the listener is attentive and genuinely interested in what they are trying to communicate. In North American culture, attentiveness to another includes eye contact, facing the person, avoiding distractions, and allowing time for them to speak without interruption. Ways to open a conversation with a student when their emotions are regulated could be:

1. You seem...
2. You appear....
3. It seems like....

You must pay attention to the content, the feelings, and the context. The content is obvious, the words used, and their meanings. Feelings may be stated or implied. The context is any material you are aware of that is related to the communication but isn't explicitly stated, including where it is being said and other information the student has related to you in the past (Buffington et al., 2016).

Reflective Feeling

Associated with reflective listening is reflective feeling. It is listening to another and then naming the emotions they are verbally or non-verbally expressing in your own words. Since younger students may not have the language to verbally express their feelings regarding a situation, reflecting feeling allows you to determine the feeling and then state it, or reflect it back, to the student. This brings greater awareness of feelings to those who do not yet have the vocabulary. There is a good reflective listening tool called the Feelings Wheel for Kids and Adults.[7]

1. Type in 'www.imom.com.'
2. In the search bar, type in 'Feel Wheel for Kids and Adults.'

Sometimes feelings are more important than content. Feeling reflections might begin with the following:

1. You sound/you're sounding …
2. You look/you're looking …
3. You feel/you're feeling …

Remember that feelings may be stated or implied. If implied, you must label them so the student can recognize them more clearly and then follow through by allowing the student to confirm that you have identified their feelings correctly. While the student is speaking, notice physical signs like body language, facial expressions, and energy. Also, pay attention to verbal signs like the tone of voice, the volume, the rate of speech, inflections, feeling words used, and, of course, content (nugget). Let's look at an example of reflective listening from *Everybody Loves Raymand Uses Active Listening*.[8] Or complete the following steps:

1. Go to YouTube.
2. Search for '*Everybody Loves Raymond Uses Active Listening*' from ParentEffectiveness Training.

Before moving on to CBT: Brain→Body, let's check for understanding with two quick scenarios followed by debriefs.

Scenario 1

Peter (breaks his pencil and raises his voice): '*This is so stupid. I'm not doing this.*' After Mrs. Yin uses a soothing voice and gives Peter the option to engage in calming activities in the chill-out area, she notices his breathing is slower, his muscles are less tense, and his face is more relaxed. She then approaches Peter.

Mrs. Yin: '*Peter, tell me a bit about how you felt about the journal entry I asked you to do. Seems you were very frustrated since you thought it was pretty stupid.*'

Peter: '*Yeah, I felt super frustrated, and I can't do it.*'

Mrs. Yin: '*Sounds like you were overwhelmed because there was something about the journal entry you couldn't do.*'

Peter:	*'Everyone else was writing a lot, and I don't know how to spell the words I want to write.'*
Mrs. Yin:	*'That does sound frustrating and overwhelming.'*
Peter:	*'You understand!'*
Mrs. Yin:	Notices that Peter's muscles relax, and his breathing is deeper.

Debrief

Mrs. Yin is reflecting back on what she hears Peter saying, without judgment. The understanding, acceptance, and validation of the situation contribute to 'attachment' between the two. The release of oxytocin that occurs during an exchange that validates the other person contributes to emotional regulation. Also, labeling Peter's feelings helps to clarify the situation so that he can gain insight into his response to the situation. A continuation of reflective listening may lead to problem-solving.

Scenario 2

Todd pushed Chad down on the playground during the noontime break. The duty monitor brought him into the office, where he sat near the administrative assistant who had soothing music playing. While Todd waits for the Vice Principal, he chooses a stress ball from the container on the counter and squeezes it. After 20 minutes, Ms. Oran arrives. She takes Todd into an empty meeting room where they can sit face-to-face without a desk between them.

Ms. Oran:	*'It sounds like you became very upset today on the playground.'*
Todd:	*'I got really angry, and I didn't know how to get Chad to stop being mean to me.'*
Ms. Oran:	*'Chad was doing or saying something that hurt your feelings.'*
Todd:	*'Yeah, he kept saying I can't read because I go to the resource room every day.'*
Ms. Oran:	*'You felt that was mean; seems like you felt he was making fun of you.'*
Todd:	*'It embarrasses me; I go to resource because I get more work done there. He made me really mad because what he is saying is not true.'*

Ms. Oran: *'Sounds like you got angry that he is saying you can't read and that is not the truth.'*

Todd (with tears in his eyes): *'Yeah. I had to get him to stop, and I couldn't find the right words to tell him. I am embarrassed that I pushed him.'*

Ms. Oran: *'You got very upset at Chad, and you couldn't find the words to tell him how you feel, so you pushed him to get him to stop.'*

Todd: *'Yes. You get it'* (Todd relaxes).

Debrief

Ms. Oran deliberately kept Todd waiting so that he had time to metabolize the cortisol and adrenaline that was released when he got angry. Furthermore, the stress balls are an intentional addition to the office front desk. They both provided an opportunity for him to contract and relax his muscles, helping to activate his PNS, 'rest and digest' system. When Ms. Oran began to speak with him, he was able to engage the rational, thinking part of his brain that was 'hijacked' during the pushing incident on the playground. She took Todd to a neutral environment, faced him without a desk between them, and listened without judgment. As she reflected back on the meaning of what she heard him say, she allowed him to clarify if what she was hearing was correct. The respect and trust built during the exchange released oxytocin, which contributes to emotional regulation. This may create a space of safety where problem-solving and learning can occur.

CBT: Brain→Body

Recognizing and Challenging Thoughts

Note we are now going in the other direction, that is to say, brain to body. Let's revisit the CBT triad. As discussed, when a student's feelings are dysregulated, they cannot think rationally or problem-solve. As a result, they are unable to recognize irrational thoughts that may be contributing to the distressed feelings. We know that engaging in sensory activities and behaviors can calm distressed thoughts; then students can identify problematic

FIGURE 5.6 Diagram Relating Thoughts, Feelings, Behaviors with Arrows

thoughts they tend to have that could lead to their emotional dysregulation.

The following scenario illustrates how different thoughts regarding an event or situation create different feelings:

> Kaitlynn and Marie-Eve were on the playground at noon time, organizing a game. Normally, their friend Heidi plays with them, but today, she walked by them and went to the basketball court without speaking to them.

Kaitlynn thought, '*Heidi is mad at me; she doesn't want to be my friend anymore.*' Kaitlynn attempted to figure out what she did wrong to upset Heidi. As she focused on the thought that it was her fault that Heidi ignored them, her mood spiraled. She could not focus on her school work in the afternoon, felt confused, and had a pain in her stomach. The relationship between Heidi's thoughts, feelings, and behaviors are visually represented in Figure 5.7.

Marie-Eve, on the other hand, thought, '*Heidi is having a quiet day; something must have happened to upset her.*' Marie-Eve set up the game and played with Kaitlynn. At the end of lunch break, she thought, '*I will ask Heidi to walk home with me to make sure she's okay*' (Figure 5.8).

Marie-Eve engaged in her schoolwork in the afternoon and, at the end of the day, asked Heidi to walk home with her. Although Kaitlynn and Marie-Eve experienced the same situation, their thoughts were different. As a result, they had different feelings and behaviors.

All people have automatic thoughts regarding themselves, others, and the future because of their life experiences. Sometimes,

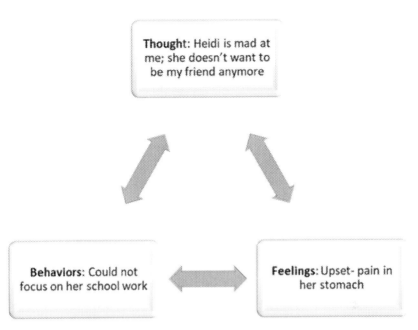

FIGURE 5.7 Kaitlynn's Thoughts/Feelings/Behaviors Regarding Heidi's Behavior

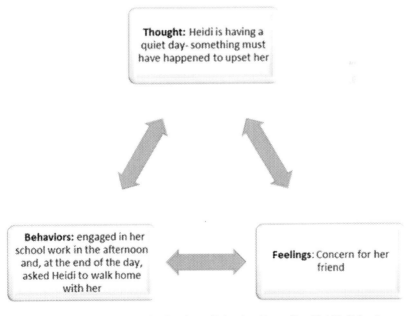

FIGURE 5.8 Marie-Eve's Thoughts/Feelings/Behaviors Regarding Heidi's Behavior

automatic thoughts are irrational or unhelpful, which may contribute to negative feelings. Dr. David Burns has created a list of common cognitive distortions[9] to be aware of. Hard-copy readers should follow these steps:

Step 1: Search for 'List of Cognitive Distortions pdf.'
Step 2: The 'Arkansas Families First, LLC' site and the 'Therapist Aid' site are similar so you can pick either (Figure 5.9).

As students learn to identify and challenge unhelpful thoughts, they gain a skill to help them regulate their emotions. Teachers can use CBT approaches in the classroom by teaching their students about irrational, unhelpful thoughts and how to challenge them. These activities, as presented in Figure 5.10 could be incorporated into the Health or Language Arts curriculum (nugget)).

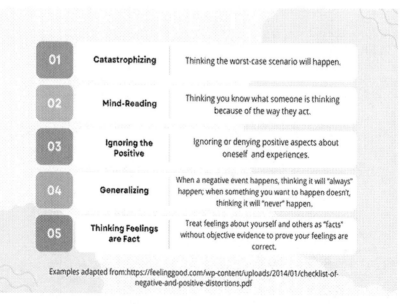

01	Catastrophizing	Thinking the worst-case scenario will happen.
02	Mind-Reading	Thinking you know what someone is thinking because of the way they act.
03	Ignoring the Positive	Ignoring or denying positive aspects about oneself and experiences.
04	Generalizing	When a negative event happens, thinking it will "always" happen; when something you want to happen doesn't, thinking it will "never" happen.
05	Thinking Feelings are Fact	Treat feelings about yourself and others as "facts" without objective evidence to prove your feelings are correct.

Examples adapted from:https://feelinggood.com/wp-content/uploads/2014/01/checklist-of-negative-and-positive-distortions.pdf

FIGURE 5.9 Examples of Unhelpful Thoughts

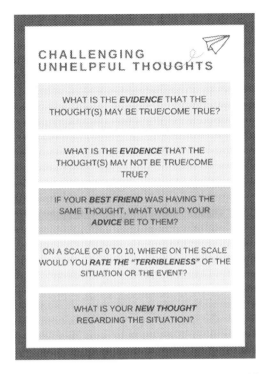

FIGURE 5.10 Techniques to Challenge Unhelpful Thoughts (Adapted by author Dr. Lori Brown, a former student of Dr. David Burns, 2005)

Break Time #5A! Practice Challenging Unhelpful Thoughts
Think of a situation or event that caused you to become frustrated, overwhelmed, or stressed. What were your thoughts and feelings? What type of unhelpful thought(s) were you engaging in? Follow the labels in diagram 5.11 to fill in Figure 5.12. We have added an 'Emotions Wheel' from Kairosgame.com (Figure 5.13) to assist you. Questions follow Figure 5.13.

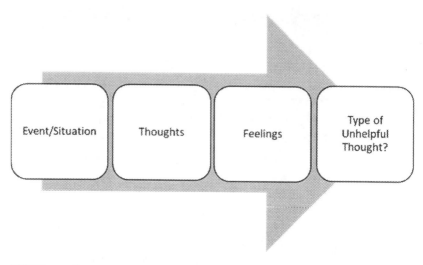

FIGURE 5.11 Events or Situations Influence Thoughts and Feelings

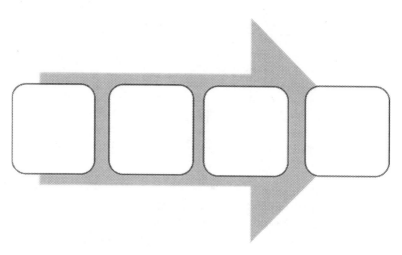

FIGURE 5.12 Events/Situations Result in Blank Template to Fill in Thoughts/Feelings/Behaviors

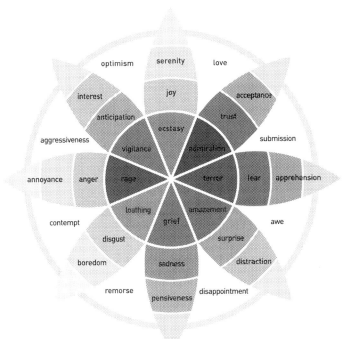

FIGURE 5.13 Emotions Wheel: Examples of Emotions to Label Feelings

a. Fill in the chart as modeled in Figure 5.11.
b. What is the evidence that your thoughts are true?
c. What is the evidence that your thoughts are *not* true?
d. If your *best friend* was having the same thought, what would your *advice* be to them?
e. On a scale of 0 to 100, where on the scale would you *rate* the 'terribleness' of the situation or the event?
f. Were there any aspects that were *positive* or a learning experience?
g. What are your new thoughts regarding the situation?
h. What are your new feelings?

Social-Emotional Learning (SEL) for Your K–3 Students

Since the concept of 'thoughts' may be too abstract for young students, showing this video, called *Mindfulness for Kids – Learning About Our Thoughts*,[10] will be helpful.

Go to YouTube. Search for *'Learning About Our Thoughts'* from Fablefy – The Whole Child.

When determining the thoughts that lead to particular feelings and vice versa, pictures of faces of different emotions can be used for pre-reading students to make the connection between their thoughts and feelings. You can use a blank outline of a body, like the one we showed earlier from the Therapist Aid, 'Where Do I Feel?' for the students to color the part of their bodies where they have specific feelings. The colors they choose are unique to them, so the color red does not have to equate to anger.

Social stories may be useful to demonstrate cognitive distortion, how different thoughts about the same situation can create different feelings. Attaching types of thoughts to different animals may be more engaging for them, as shown at CBT Animals.[11] Simply follow the steps:

1. Go to Google.
2. Search 'CBT Animals' from Squarespace.

There you will find a free download that has posters, stories, and activities to encourage students in grades K–3 to recognize how their thoughts can lead to specific feelings and vice versa. You can change the animals to make them more culturally relevant. You may then wish to translate the names, although this will affect the alliterations like 'Toxic Tiger.'

Social-Emotional Learning (SEL) for Your Grade 4–6 Students

The activities that demonstrate ways to identify thoughts that are not helpful and replace them with more rational thoughts can be found at CBT Behavior Worksheets[12] or follow the steps:

1. Go to Google.
2. Type in 'CBT Worksheets' and look for the site PositiveKids.ca.

There you will find a free download that contains a CBT program for this grade range. The program includes hands-on activities and information for teaching about the connection between thoughts, feelings, and behaviors. The categories are as follows:

1. Emotional Rating Scales
2. Think-Feel-Act Sheets
3. Problem-Solving Road Maps

We are including some links to other resources for SEL at the back of the chapter.

Scenario 3

Miranda is in grade 4. Her teacher, Mr. Yani, has noticed a pattern in Miranda's relationships with the other students. Miranda makes friends with the girls in her class, and within a few weeks, there is a 'falling out,' and she will not sit near the former 'friend.' Mr. Yani has had some conversations with Miranda after class. He notices that Miranda feels others sometimes 'look at her the wrong way' or are rude to her. She is very sensitive to people 'slighting' her.

Mr. Yani referred Miranda's situation to the School Team who included the school psychologist and counselor. They recommended a series of classroom visits where they would talk about how thoughts, feelings, and behaviors affect one another and how types of thoughts, while they can make us feel a certain way, do not dictate what is reality. The counselor and psychologist would spend each visit discussing one particular type of cognitive distortion, leave a poster, and provide Mr. Yani with a few activities to reiterate the concepts. They would model and teach ways to identify and challenge irrational thoughts to make space for more rational ones while paying attention to how more rational thoughts change one's mood.

With this new knowledge, Miranda might be able to self-identify as 'Mind Reading' and then challenge these thoughts and recognize that she, in fact, doesn't know what the other students are really thinking. She could learn to ask herself, 'Is there evidence that they don't like me?' 'Is there evidence that the way they looked was about me?' Hopefully, by challenging her cognitive distortions, Miranda could develop more rational thoughts and feelings about her peers.

CBT for Teachers

As teachers, we can use the thoughts-behaviors-feelings triad as a powerful tool to keep ourselves grounded. Educators have dozens of important decisions to make every day, most of which we cannot plan for; this can lead to triggering the stress response. Although our PFC is developed, arming us with greater foresight, problem-solving skills, and judgment than our students' have, our amygdala will be activated at times. As we know, when the stress response is set in motion, foresight, judgment, and problem-solving are compromised. How can we use the powerful CBT triad to prevent the amygdala from initiating the cascade of hormones that make us confused, sweaty, nauseous, and unable to express ourselves effectively?

Brain Break #5B: CBT for the Teacher!

Jane is a first-year teacher at Lakeside Elementary School. She has been evaluated by her department head and Principal; the evaluation will determine whether the School District will renew her contract for the following school year.

Jane received a rating of 4 out of 5 on professionalism, organization, and subject knowledge. She received a 3 out of 5 on communication with her students' guardians. The comments stated specific observations to validate her strengths while including a short sentence encouraging her to communicate more often with guardians.

Jane has options:

Option #1: *'I lost points in all categories of my evaluation. I guess I am not a good teacher, and obviously, my administration does not like me. I will not get my contract renewed, so I might as well start looking for a new job.'*

She feels confused, defeated, discouraged, and inadequate.

Option #2: *'As a first-year teacher, 4 out of 5 in professionalism, organization, and subject knowledge is pretty good. I am glad my administration appreciates these aspects of my teaching. It is easy for me to connect with guardians more frequently because I am now more efficient. If I need to apply to teach at another school, this is a great evaluation to take with me!'*

She feels hopeful, appreciated, and respected.

◆ Was option #1 helpful and based on evidence?
◆ If we look back at the types of cognitive distortions that we all engage in from time to time, what types of distortions was Jane engaging in?

Brain Break #5C: CBT for the Teacher!
Raj, a grade 4 teacher, woke up late on a school day. He argued with his partner the night before, so he is rushed and tired. Although he has 24 students in the class, Johnny, who is often upset, seems to take most of his time.

So, Raj has options:

Option #1: *'Things would be so much easier today if Johnny wasn't at school. I don't think I can deal with his up-and-down feelings today. I am going to ask the Student Assistant to take him for a long walk during class time.'*

He feels irritated, overwhelmed, and annoyed.

Option #2: *'I wonder if Johnny had a hard evening and morning as well. I am going to have a chat with him before class so we can both arm ourselves with stress balls. I'll model the deep breathing as I am using the stress ball during class. We'll be in this together.'* Johnny has lots of practice with deep breathing and stress balls are his 'go-to' when he is feeling distressed.

He feels playful, caring, and compassionate.

◆ Was option #1 helpful?
◆ What are the consequences of thought #1 compared to thought #2?

Identifying our thoughts can be tricky. As soon as we have uncomfortable feelings, we can try to identify them. If we identify them as irrational thoughts, we can use techniques to challenge them.

Your knowledge of CBT should not end here. Learn from your guidance counselor or school psychologist, and plan professional development around this important topic. CBT offers practical strategies to enhance your students' self-regulation. The strategies can be continually improved upon throughout the year. You know you have been successful in fostering insight and empathy when you see your students coaching each other. CBT can transform your learning environment by adding adaptability and resilience to your students' list of strengths. They will require these two traits for use in the world they will be entering as adults.

Answers to Brain Breaks

Break Time #5A! Practice Challenging Unhelpful Thoughts

1. We are providing answers to a fictitious situation. Your answers will differ but should follow the same pattern (Figure 5.14).

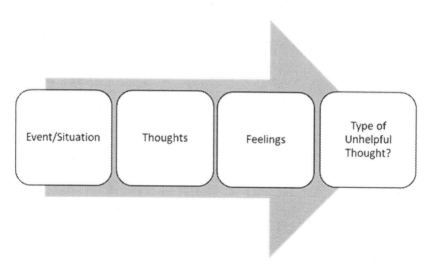

FIGURE 5.14 Events or Situations Influence Thoughts and Feelings

a) Fill in the chart as modeled in Figure 5.14.

Situation/Event	Thoughts	Feelings	Types of Unhelpful Thought
Katrina, a grade 4 student, disrupts the class again.	'Katrina is being disrespectful; she always disrupts the other students' learning.'	Annoyed Frustrated Resentful	1. Generalizing 2. Mindreading 3. Treating Feelings as Facts 4. Ignoring the Positive

b) What is the evidence that your thoughts are true?
Although I think and feel Katrina is being disrespectful, she may not view her actions as not respecting others. Also, there are situations in which Katrina does not interrupt others, so she does not 'always' disrupt others' learning.

c) What is the evidence that your thoughts are *not* true?
I notice that when Katrina is in math or art, she rarely disrupts the class, so she is not 'always' disrupting others.

During unstructured time at school, Katrina is kind and helpful; she has positive interactions with others.

d) If your *best friend* was having the same thought, what would your *advice* be to them?
Since she does not behave this way in all her classes, there may be something about the subject or learning activities that prevents her from focusing. Even though her behavior appears to be disrespectful, she does not have a disrespectful personality – it may be important to explore her thoughts and feelings leading up to the disruptive behaviors.

e) On a scale of 0 to 100, where on the scale would you *rate* the 'terribleness' of the situation or the event?
The disruptions are annoying and frustrating to me but may be indicative of a need Katrina is trying to fulfill and communicate. A referral to the School Team, a discussion with her previous teacher, and a conversation with

Katrina's guardians may give some insight to help fulfill her needs at school. There are many other resources to help with this situation. Looking at it this way makes it seems manageable and solvable. Since it is a frequent issue that pops up with many students, it is really only a 4 out of 10 in terms of 'terribleness' at this point.

f) Were there any aspects that were *positive* or a learning experience?
I reminded myself that this student has many assets.

g) What are your new thoughts regarding the situation?
I can have a School Team and her parents help me find out the reasons Katrina is blurting things out in class. This behavior doesn't happen in other situations, and Katrina is not intentionally trying to be disrespectful.

h) What are your new feelings?
Curious, empathetic, hopeful

Brain Break #5B: CBT for the Teacher!

Jane is a first-year teacher at Lakeside Elementary School. She has been evaluated by her department head and Principal; the evaluation will determine whether the School District will renew her contract for the following school year.

Jane received a rating of 4 out of 5 on professionalism, organization, and subject knowledge. She received a 3 out of 5 on communication with her students' guardians. The comments stated specific observations to validate her strengths while including a short sentence encouraging her to communicate more often with guardians.

Jane has options:

Option #1: *'I lost points in all categories of my evaluation. I guess I am not a good teacher, and obviously, my administration does not like me. I will not get my contract*
Renewed, so I might as well start looking for a new job.'

She feels confused, defeated, discouraged, and inadequate.

Option #2: 'As a first-year teacher, 4 out of 5 in professionalism, organization, and subject knowledge is pretty good. I am glad my administration appreciates these aspects of my teaching. It is easy for me to connect with guardians more frequently because I am now more efficient. If I need to apply to teach at another school, this is a great evaluation to take with me!'

She feels hopeful, appreciated, and respected.

---

a. Was option #1 helpful and based on evidence?
   Jane's thoughts disregarded the positive aspects of her evaluation. There was no evidence that her administrator did not like her and no rational reason to believe her contract would not be renewed.
b. If we look back at the types of cognitive distortions that we all engage in from time to time, what types of distortions was Jane engaging in?
   Catastrophizing, Mind Reading, Discounting the Positive, Overgeneralizing

---

Brain Break #5C: CBT for the Teacher!
Raj, a grade 4 teacher, woke up late on a school day. He argued with his partner the night before, so he is rushed and tired. Although he has 24 students in the class, Johnny, who is often upset, seems to take most of his time.

So, Raj has options:

Option #1: 'Things would be so much easier today if Johnny wasn't at school. I don't think I can deal with his up-and-down feelings today. I am going to ask the Student Assistant to take him for a long walk during class time.'

He feels irritated, overwhelmed, and annoyed.

Option #2: '*I wonder if Johnny had a hard evening and morning as well. I am going to have a chat with him before class so we can both arm ourselves with stress balls. I'll model the deep breathing as I am using the stress ball during class. We'll "be in this together."*' Johnny has lots of practice with deep breathing, and stress balls are his 'go-to' when he is feeling distressed.

He feels playful, caring, and compassionate.

> a. Was option #1 helpful?
> No, Raj engaged in catastrophizing and anticipating Johnny's behavior as being time-consuming without really knowing. This led to Raj having irritated and overwhelming feelings before even interacting with Johnny. This is not fair to Johnny.
> b. What are the consequences of thought #1 compared to thought #2?
> Thought #2 reveals a trusting relationship that has developed between Raj and his student. His understanding and caring thoughts, as well as knowledge of what soothes Johnny, led to playful, caring, and compassionate feelings.

Notes

1 https://www.youtube.com/watch?v=oyS6a-t0ToU.
2 https://www.youtube.com/watch?v=gd65sMGERrU&t=5s.
3 https://www.youtube.com/watch?v=30VMlEmA114.
4 https://www.therapistaid.com/therapy-worksheet/where-do-i-feel.
5 https://sesameworkshop.org/search?s=I+notice+I+feel+I+can.
6 https://kairosgame.com/en/emotion-wheel.
7 https://www.imom.com/printable/printable-feelings-wheel/.
8 https://www.youtube.com/watch?v=4VOubVB4CTU.

9 https://arfamiliesfirst.com/wp-content/uploads/2013/05/Cognitive-Distortions.pdf.

10 https://www.youtube.com/watch?v=HHm5DzlU9as.

11 https://static1.squarespace.com/static/635a1360b5d4b729bdb834f2/t/63d2d7a2e89f285ac4481fe3/1674762163351/CBT+Cognitive+Distortion+Animals.pdf.

12 https://positivekids.ca/wp-content/uploads/2021/01/CBT-worksheets.pdf.

Resources

What Is the CBT Triangle? (https://www.therapistaid.com/therapy-worksheet/cbt-for-kids/cbt/children)

Worksheets: Free download CBT Workbook for Children (https://www.teacherspayteachers.com/Product/Free-Worksheets-from-CBT-Toolbox-for-Children-and-Adolescents-4316464)

Thinking Errors (worksheet) | Therapist Aid (https://www.therapistaid.com/therapy-worksheet/cbt-thinking-errors/cbt/children)

Sammy Sloths Unhelpful Thoughts Story (https://shop.thecounselingteacher.com/collections/printed-and-shipped-products/products/sammy-sloths-unhelpful-thoughts-paperback-book-pre-order)

Thought Challenging Exercise (https://www.mylemarks.com/store/p873/The_Size_of_My_Problem_%28_ES%29.html)

De-escalating Challenging Behaviours (https://performex-consulting.com/)

References

Arnold, A. (2014). Behind the mirror: Reflective listening and its tain in the work of Carl Rogers. *The Humanistic Psychologist, 42*, 354–369.

Baweja, S., Santiago, C., Vona, P., Pears, J., Langley, A., & Kataoka, S. (2016). Improving implementation of a school-based program for traumatized students: Identifying factors that promote teacher support and collaboration. *School Mental Health, 8,* 120–131.

Beck, A. T. (2019). A 60-year evolution of cognitive theory and therapy. *Perspectives on Science, 14*(1), 16–20. https://doi.org/10.11772F1745691618804187

Buffington, A., Wenner, P., Brandenburg, D., Berge, J., Sherman, M., & Danner, C. (2016). The art of listening. *Minnesota Medicine, 99*(6), 46–48.

Burns, D. D. (2005). Overview of 50 cognitive distortions. Feeling Good. https://feelinggood.com/wp-content/uploads/2018/05/b2a45-overview-of-50-cbt-techniques-version-of-2005.pdf

Csikszentmihalyi, M. (2003). *Flow.* Into the Classroom Media. Springer.

De Manzano, Ö., Cervenka, S., Jucaite, A., Hellenäs, O., Farde, L., & Ullén, F. (2013). Individual differences in the proneness to have flow experiences are linked to dopamine D2-receptor availability in the dorsal striatum. *NeuroImage, 67,* 1–6.

Esther, D., Pollio, E., Cooper, B., & Steer, R. A. (2020). Disseminating trauma-focused cognitive behavioral therapy with a systematic self-care approach to addressing secondary traumatic stress: Practice what you preach. *Community Mental Health Journal, 56*(8), 1531–1543. http://doi.org/proxy1.calsouthern.edu/10.1007/s10597-020-00602-x

Levine, P. A. (2010). *In an unspoken voice: How the body releases trauma and restores goodness.* North Atlantic Books.

RB-Banks, Y., & Meyer, J. (2017). Childhood trauma in today's urban classroom moving beyond the therapist's office. *The Journal of Educational Foundations, 30*(4), 63–75.

Reilly, E., Gunnar, M. (2019). Neglect, HPA axis reactivity, and development. *International Journal of Developmental Neuroscience, 78,* 100–108. doi: 10.1016/j.ijdevneu.2019.07.010. Epub 2019 Jul 30. PMID: 31374220.

Santiago, C. D., Raviv, T., Ros, A. M., Brewer, S. K., Distel, L. M. L., Torres, S. A., Fuller, A. K., Lewis, K. M., Coyne, C. A., Cicchetti, C., & Langley, A. K. (2018). Implementing the bounce back trauma intervention in urban elementary schools: A real-world replication trial. *School Psychology Quarterly, 33*(1), 1–9. https://doi.org/10.1037/spq0000229

6

Conclusions

Embracing *trauma-informed* strategies in education has to go beyond the buzzword that it now is. It must signify a genuine commitment to recognizing and addressing your students' traumas as a necessary stepping stone to their education.

By drawing on the work of leaders in their fields, as well as valuable online resources, we aimed to enhance your awareness of the multiple causes and impacts that ACEs have on your students. We embedded over 30 nuggets, over 25 websites to visit, and YouTube videos to watch, as well as 11 Brain Breaks because we wanted this book to extend beyond just a few hours of reading. Hopefully, it will serve as an ongoing valuable resource for implementing new standards in your classroom.

We have covered a lot, from basic facts about how the nervous system functions to cognitive behavior therapy for the stressed-out teacher. We hope that the last chapter in this book is not the last chapter you ever read in your trauma-informed education. Lean on experts in your school and your district, and reach out to experts in the field. Your little charges are so much more than the ACEs they are trying to cope with, as are you. By creating the environments we described in this book, you are arming your students with the skills and knowledge they need to reach their full potential and become healthy, contributing members of their society.

DOI: 10.4324/9781032707945-9